The Aboriginal Population Of The North Coast Of California

by

S. F. Cook

The Aboriginal Population Of The North Coast Of California
by S. F. Cook

ISBN: 978-93-59953-88-5

Published by

DOUBLE 9 BOOKS

2/13-B, Ansari Road
Daryaganj, New Delhi – 110002
info@double9books.com
www.double9books.com
Tel. 011-40042856

ABOUT THE AUTHOR

S. F. Cook, the accomplished creator of "The Aboriginal Population of Alameda and Contra Costa Counties, California," stands as a high-quality determine inside the realm of historical and demographic literature. This work is frequently appeared as considered one of his masterpieces, reflecting his determination to bridging the nation-states of history and demography. With a notable pen and a profound expertise of his subjects, Cook excels in elucidating the complex historical and demographic elements of the indigenous populations in Alameda and Contra Costa Counties. His writings transcend mere data and information, facilitating a deeper connection amongst readers and fostering a superior understanding of both the past and the folks who inhabit those areas. Cook's literary prowess is a testomony to his creativity and ardour. He invitations readers on a fascinating journey thru numerous landscapes and emotions, painting vibrant pix together with his phrases. His writing style is a brilliant fusion of beauty and accessibility, making his extraordinary tales a satisfaction for readers of all backgrounds and interests. S. F. Cook's contributions to the literary global expand beyond his understanding in historical and demographic studies; his capacity to train, inspire, and connect people via the pages of his books ensures that his legacy endures as an enriching and enlightening pressure within the world of literature.

CONTENTS

INTRODUCTION

The present manuscript attempts a reassessment of the aboriginal population of Northwestern California, from the Oregon line to the Bay of San Francisco. There are no natural and fixed limits to the territory. Its outline serves merely the purposes of convenience. For this reason the individual units within the whole area are based, not upon natural ecological provinces such as mountain ranges, valleys, or river basins, but upon ethnic or "tribal" boundaries. Moreover, since there is no necessary interrelationship between the component parts, each is considered as a separate entity, and its population is computed separately. There is no final grand total to be added up, the significance of which transcends that of any of the constituents.

Since the objective here is the calculation of pure numbers, it is irrelevant that the natural habitat, the mode of life, the reactions to environment of the various tribes and linguistic stocks vary enormously. Such a disregard for the basic principles of ethnography and human ecology will be tolerated only because the limitations of space and time demand that the fundamental question "What *was* the population?" be answered before opening up the problem of *why* the population was no greater or no less. We must know how many people there were before we can study their equilibrium with the physical or cultural environment.

The outcome of this study is to augment markedly the previously estimated number of inhabitants in the region at hand, and, by implication, the number in the whole state. The magnitude of the aboriginal population has steadily diminished in our eyes for many years. I believe it was Powers who thought that the natives numbered as high as 750,000 or more. Merriam thought there were 260,000. Kroeber, in the Handbook of California Indians, (1925, p. 882) reduced it to 133,000. I myself in an earlier work (1943, pp. 161 *et seq.*) reviewed the evidence and raised Kroeber's figure by no more than 10 per cent. It appears to me that the trend toward assessing the native population in continually diminishing terms is due to the operation of two factors.

The first is a tendency on the part of subsequent generations to adopt a highly skeptical attitude toward all statements and testimony derived from earlier generations. Inherent in this point of view is the feeling, consciously expressed or unconsciously followed, that all human beings contemporary with an event either lie deliberately or exaggerate without compunction. This failing, so the argument runs, becomes most apparent when any numerical estimates are involved. Thus the soldier inevitably grossly magnifies the force of the enemy, the priest inflates the number of his flock, the farmer falsifies the size of his herds, the woodsman increases the height of the tree—all just as the fisherman enlarges upon the big one which got away. That these individuals are frequently subject to an urge to exaggerate cannot for a moment be denied. Nevertheless, under many circumstances most men lack a desire to do so or, if they feel such desire, know how to curb it.

To maintain explicitly or by implication that every observer without exception who reported on the size of Indian villages or the numbers of Indians seen was guilty of inflating the values is no more justifiable than to accuse every man who makes a tax return of having cheated the government. Under our law each person is innocent until proved guilty. Similarly, within the range of his intellect and the scope of his senses a traveler or a settler or a miner or a soldier of one hundred years ago should be credited with telling the truth unless there is clear evidence from outside sources that he is prevaricating. Evidence of falsehood should be looked for and, if found, the account should be discounted or discredited. Otherwise it should be admitted at face value. It need not be stressed, of course, that the acceptance or the rejection of a given datum because it does or does not conform to a preconceived theory constitutes a major scientific crime.

In the assessment of the California population it may have come about through the years that the disinclination to agree with contemporary observation has been carried too far and that a more liberal attitude of mind is needed. If so, then the reduction of the population which has taken place in print may have overshot its mark and the figures may require revision upwards.

The second factor is methodological. Throughout the last half-century, and beginning with the pioneer work of Barrett and Kroeber, ethnographers have employed the informant method almost exclusively. It is not my intention to deprecate this procedure in any way or to imply that it has not proved an exceedingly valuable tool. I would like to suggest, however that it does carry certain limitations. I refer specifically to the inability of old men and women to remember and transmit *quantitative* facts over a great span of years. On the other hand, *qualitative* facts and ideas can persist in the mind with little or no blurring or alteration. Thus a man might retain clearly from his own memory, or through that of his parents, *where* a village was located, what its *name* was, and some of the *people* who lived there.

Yet he might have no clear concept whatever *how many* persons inhabited the village or *how many* villages were known to the tribe. This failure to retain and transmit accurate knowledge of number or mensuration becomes intensified if the informant is required to reach across an intervening period of unrest and confusion, both physical and mental, to an era of stability long since vanished. Yet this is just what the informant is asked to do when he tries to tell about the geographic and demographic conditions existing one or more generations prior to his own youth.

I do not wish to advocate throwing out all informant testimony for these reasons—or, indeed, any of it. I merely wish to suggest that an undeviating adherence to literal statements of informants may on occasion lead to population estimates which are too low. The same discretion and criticism should be accorded them as in the other direction should be accorded to the statements left by contemporary white observers.

THE YUROK

The first exhaustive and scholarly attempt to assess aboriginal population was that of A. L. Kroeber (1925) in his Handbook of the Indians of California. He made a particularly careful study of and worked out his fundamental principles with the Yurok. Hence any reappraisement of the population problem in Northwest California must begin with a thorough examination of all the evidence pertaining to this tribe.

Three primary avenues of approach are possible: ecological, ethnographic, and archaeological. It is proposed to deal here with the second, or ethnographic material. The principal sources are three in number; the pertinent chapter in the Handbook, the extensive monograph by Waterman (1920) and the village lists of Merriam (see Bibliography). All these investigators inspected the terrain and interviewed many informants during the decade 1900-1910. Hence their data have now become definitive.

For calculating population from village data it is necessary to know the number of houses per village and the number of inhabitants per house. Both these variables depend for their value upon numerous demographic and cultural factors and hence must be determined separately for nearly every tribe studied. Kroeber has paid special attention to the second variable, the number of inhabitants per house, and has concluded that the best value for the Yurok is 7.5 persons. Since all the contemporary accounts agree with this conclusion it may be accepted as established.

With regard to the number of houses per village it must be admitted that this factor is subject to wide variation both in locality and time. The number of house pits observed many years after the village itself has disappeared is likely to be unreliable for many reasons, although it may be used as a first approximation in default of better data. A safer guide is the memory of reliable informants or actual house counts made by explorers or original settlers. These are the sources of the values given by Kroeber and Waterman.

For the Yurok there are five chief compilations of villages, with and without house counts:

1. *Kroeber*. This author shows (1925, p. 18) a list of fifteen villages (four of them compound) which he says are "recent counts of houses or house pits recollected as inhabited." In addition he shows on his map a number of other towns, some of which he regards, and so designates, as being temporarily or intermittently inhabited and hence not to be included in any computation of permanent population. The house counts from his list are shown in table 2 (p. 92, herein) in the column headed "Kroeber, *modern memories*."

2. *Kroeber*. given a census for the fifteen villages mentioned above. This was made in 1852 by a "trader" named York who lived many years in the vicinity. The census has all the appearance of veracity and may be accepted as substantially accurate. It is shown in table 2 (p. 92, herein) in the column headed "Kroeber, *1852 census*".

3. *Waterman*. This author presents his findings, all from informants, in three ways. First are his textual descriptions, which are careful and circumstantial. Second are his maps of a few villages, on which the house locations are drawn with much detail. Third there is the summarizing list, in which most of the textual and other data are incorporated. With respect to house counts there are numerous discrepancies between text, list, and maps, some of which are difficult to reconcile. Since from the context it may be inferred that the list represents Waterman's final evaluation, it must be used as the basic source of information.

4. *Waterman*. With the list is also given a list of villages derived from a map executed by a man named Randall, a county surveyor, in 1866. Although no house counts are given, the list is useful for establishing the existence of certain towns in the year 1866.

5. *Merriam*. The village lists for the Yurok follow Waterman and Kroeber quite closely. However, Merriam was able to locate several inhabited places which had escaped the attention of the other two investigators. These villages have been added in table 2 (p. 92, herein) and a conservatively estimated house count assigned to them.

In table 1 (pp. 85-91, herein) will be found a list of 78 villages, based primarily on Waterman's data. Under each village name are assembled such facts as I can find in the writings of Kroeber and Waterman bearing on the existence of the town. In the third column is placed my own evaluation of these facts in the form of a statement whether such existence should be regarded as certain, probable, or doubtful. The results have been then transferred to table 2 (p. 92, herein). In the first column of this second table is the arbitrary number assigned each town shown in table 1 (pp. 85-91, herein), the doubtful towns being omitted. In the second column is the source, where the letter "l" denotes that the house number is derived from Waterman's list, the letter "t" that the number was derived from Waterman's textual descriptions, and the letter "M" that the data were secured from Merriam's village lists. The letter "R" indicates that the town appeared on Randall's map of 1866 but was not adequately discussed by Waterman or Kroeber. The letter "p" indicates that the house number is my own estimate. The third column shows the house number itself. In addition are shown the corresponding house numbers as taken from Kroeber's informants ("modern memories") or from the census of 1852 as cited by Kroeber.

The total number of houses is 412, which, at 7.5 persons per house, gives a population of 3,090.

Some insight into the validity of the value thus obtained may be secured by cross checking the various sources for house number. As a basis for comparison the list in table 1 (pp. 85-91, herein) may be used, since it is constructed for the great majority of villages from Waterman's final estimate. There are 16 towns for which a number is given in Waterman's list (1920, p. 206) and for which a statement of house numbers derived directly from informants is to be found in his detailed descriptions. For these towns the list shows 88 houses and the text 101. Now, if the same ratio of house numbers (*i.e.*, 88 to 101) is applied to the total population as derived from table 2 (p. 92, herein) the result is a population of 3,562 persons.

On his detailed maps Waterman shows the location of the houses in 19 villages. Presumably he checked these houses carefully with informants, for in many instances he appends the house names, although as a rule only the pits remained when he saw the sites. There are in all 210 houses, whereas in his list for the same towns he gives 192 houses. The total population projected from the maps would then be 3,380.

In a similar manner Waterman's list may be compared with Kroeber's list from informants and from the 1852 census. For the pertinent towns the numbers are: Waterman, 163 houses; Kroeber's informants, 154; the 1852 census 141. Projecting to the full list in table 2 (p. 91, herein) the population values are respectively 2,918 and 2,671. Of all the extrapolations the most significant is that from the 1852 census for it demonstrates that *at that date* the Yurok population could not have fallen far short of 2,500, a figure set by Kroeber as the absolute maximum for *aboriginal times*. In 1852 the tribe had already suffered materially from the disturbance caused by white settlement and hence must not have represented the full pre-settlement value. The average of all five estimates is 3,124.

Kroeber states unequivocally that he cannot concede to the Yurok a population greater than 2,500. Yet the best ethnographic data we possess, much of it assembled by Kroeber himself, indicate a population of 3,100 to 3,200. The key to the controversy seems to lie in Kroeber's decision that house sites and pits must be reduced by a factor of one-third in order to compute population. His conclusions are summed up in the following paragraph (1925, p. 18):

> The Yurok recognize that a village normally contained more named house sites than inhabited houses. Families died out, consolidated, or moved away. The pit of their dwelling remained and its name would also survive for a generation or two. If allowance is made for parts of villages washed out by floods and possibly by mining, or dwellings already abandoned when the Americans came and totally forgotten 60 years later, the number of houses sites on these 30 miles of river may be set at 200 or more in place of 173. In other words there were *two houses to each three recognized house sites* among the Yurok in native times.

Let us now consider the following points.

1. With respect to the 173 house sites mentioned in the paragraph above Kroeber states on the same "Recent counts of houses and house pits *recollected as inhabited*, total over 170 for the Rekwoi-Kepel stretch." (Emphasis mine.) In other words the data furnished by Kroeber's informants and presented in the table were not based upon the actual or presumptive number of pits but on inhabited houses. It is this total which conforms so closely to the count made by the census-takers of 1852 and also that shown on Waterman's list. By Kroeber's own admission therefore a one-third reduction for these Yurok towns would not only be unnecessary but would lead to entirely false conclusions.

2. Kroeber is not clear whether he means house pits existing on the ground in 1910 or pits which *might* have been visible had there been no destruction due to floods or mining subsequent to 1850. He states that, if the latter are included, then the number of house sites "may be set at" 200 or more. But by implication he recommends that the observed number be reduced by one-third. Now on Waterman's maps the author shows for 19 towns the actual or approximate location of the pits visible or otherwise known in the year 1909. There are 210 of these. At the same time the inhabited houses recollected by informants for the same towns, as revised by him in his list, is 192. Hence the true ratio of reduction is not one-third, or 1 in 3, but 18 in 210, or 1 in 11.7. It is of course possible to *assume* that 78 pits were destroyed between 1850 and 1909 so that the total number was 288 instead of 210. Then, if the one-third reduction is applied, the result is 192 houses. Such an arithmetical exercise constitutes merely arguing in a circle. On the basis of Waterman's concrete data it would appear reasonable to make a 10 per cent reduction in those localities where information concerning number of houses is derived exclusively from pits remaining long after habitation has ceased.

3. Certain considerations apply to absolute town size apart from the problem of house number. In Waterman's text descriptions there is no clear instance of a village inhabited in 1909 which had been settled or originated after 1850, apart from relocations due to floods or mining. On the other hand, there are numerous towns which declined or disappeared during the days of the American invasion and of which the memory was very hazy in the minds of informants sixty years later. For instance *hopaw* had been broken up by smallpox "in the early days." The village of *rnr* was being abandoned at the time of the coming of the whites. The inhabitants of *keperor* "all died at once" and the site was deserted. When Waterman saw *otsepor* the village had only three house pits, but informants well remembered several families living there. Waterman felt sure that *srpr, espaw,* and *loolego* had been larger in aboriginal times than informants seemed to think. The region around Big Lagoon was once much more populous than Waterman's data would indicate. No one of these instances is in any way conclusive but their cumulative effect is considerable. It is quite possible therefore that along the entire northwest coast and the Klamath basin the population began an abrupt decline coinciding with the first arrival of permanent white settlers. Such a condition would be in entire conformity with much of the testimony derived from informants in 1910.

TABLE 1

Analysis of Village Sites

According to Kroeber, Waterman, and Merriam. Unless otherwise specified, page numbers refer to Waterman (1920). The column "Status" indicates whether the existence of a village at or about the year 1850 may be regarded as certain (C), probable (P), or doubtful (D).

No. and name	Status	Comment
1. omen-hipur	C	Two groups of house pits. No further information available to Waterman but regarded as a town by Kroeber (map,).
2. omen	C	Four house pits but designated as a town. It was known that a sweathouse existed and that the people bathed in the sea. Hence it was inhabited within the memory of informants. Shown by Kroeber as a town (map,).
3. rekwoi	C	No question concerning this town.
4. welkwa	C	No question.
5. tsekwel	P	P. 232. "This place was mentioned as a town site," but Waterman could get no satisfactory data. Since it was mentioned specifically as a town site by informants its existence may be regarded as probable. Mentioned by Kroeber somewhat doubtfully as a separate village.
6. tmri	C	"Said to have been a village site." "Captain Jack belonged here." Hence it certainly was inhabited. The American town of Requa is located on the site and hence its organization has been lost. Kroeber states it as being somewhat doubtful as a separate village but shows it on his map as a village occupied only during certain periods.
7. awmennok	P	On Merriam's lists as a "village on north side of Klamath River at foot of Bowie's hill about 1 mile above present Requa."
8. kere	P	On Merriam's lists as a "village on south side Klamath about 2 miles from mouth."
9. kestitsa	D	See no. 11.

<u>No. and name</u>   <u>Status</u>   <u>Comment</u>

No. and name	Status	Comment
10. pegwolaw	D	See no. 11.
11. otweg	D	These three villages were "referred to" but their location not pointed out by Waterman's informants. He suggests they may have been suburbs of rekwoi. Kroeber shows otwego as an intermittently occupied village on his map and calls it somewhat doubtful as a separate village on kestitsa and pegwolaw he calls suburbs. It is clear that a constellation of villages was located here aboriginally, centered around rekwoi. Waterman in his list assigns 25 houses to rekwoi, 9 to welkwa and none to the others. Regardless of their status of independence or permanency there are too many of these remembered sites to be ignored. Consequently 3 houses each are assigned to Waterman's two best authenticated sites, tsekwei and tmri, and to Merriam's sites awmennok and kere.
12. osegen	C	A "small town." Informants recalled 3 houses and 2 sweathouses.
13. hopaw	C	"The small pox raged here in the early days and practically broke up the village." This may be a clue to the status of the sites around rekwoi. If so, all modern informants may be too low in their estimates of houses in the area.
14. wokel	C	No question.
15. trwr	C	See no. 16.
16. ahlawsl	C	According to Waterman this was a camp site. There were very old house pits dating from a time before the memory of informants at trwr. They had been all washed away in Waterman's time. Kroeber states that trwr was a camp site with no permanent houses.

No. and name	Status	Comment
		On the other hand Merriam in his village list says: Terwer was "a village on north side of Klamath at Terwer Creek (old Klamath reservation); said to be 6 or 7 miles above present Requa." It was mentioned by Taylor in 1860. Regarding ahlawsl Merriam says that it was on the north bank close to terwer and may be regarded as the lower part of the latter village. It was called alaaca by Stevens in 1868. The existence of the combined town may hence be regarded as highly probable if not certain. In view of its apparent size 8 houses may be assigned to it.
17. yaktar	P	Merriam says that this was "a village on south bank Klamath River at mouth of McGarvey Creek. Waterman gives yoxwtr-wroi as name of McGarvey Creek but says nothing as to a village at its mouth."
18. saal	C	An "important town" with 7 to 8 houses. Waterman, however, shows only 5 on his list.
19. turip	C	A "town" lying on a flat. According to Waterman it was one of two sites but he could get no information on the second site because of local hostility. Some informants said turip itself had 8 houses and 3 sweathouses. On Randall's map (see Waterman, pp. 205 ff.) there is shown a town, called koppa, on the same flat as turip. This is not likely to be an error for saal, because the latter is across the river, but is very likely Waterman's second site. Waterman houses for turip but in view of the second probable village I recommend increasing this to 8 and thus agree with Waterman's informants. Kroeber does not mention this matter.

20. stowen   P   This is a "well known place" with Indians living there now, although they are not the descendants of the ancient population. However Waterman also says, that "the site is well known and may have been a settlement in former times." Furthermore, it is on the survey map Randall made in 1866. This map appears to have been accurately drawn and creates a strong presumption that the village was in existence in early times. It is reasonable to assign 3 houses to the site.

21. rliiken-pets   C   See no. 23.

22. howego   P   See no. 23.

23. tawchter   P   There is some confusion about these three places. Kroeber shows (map,) rliiken-pets as a place occupied intermittently, but does not mention howego or tawchter. The first (rliiken-pets) is stated by Waterman to have been the "site of a small settlement" where informants recalled 2 houses and a sweathouse. In the summer the people went to howego to camp and fish. howego is described as a "flat" with no houses mentioned, but on Waterman says: "howego ... is a well known place ... but was not described to me as a town. Apparently there is an old town site there ... whose existence I did not hear of when on the spot." Further evidence lies in the fact that the place is shown on the map by Randall under the name of Herwahgah.

Merriam lists rliiken-pets as oleeken and says that it is a "former village ... about 3 miles below Blue Creek ... named from Oleeken Bar, at the upper end of which it is located." On his "Geographic List" of Yurok villages he describes Hawwagah as an "old camp" but on his later list entitled "Polikan (Yurok) Tribes, Bands and Settlements" he has interpolated in ink "former village." Tawchter he describes as a "village on north bank of Klamath right across from Hawwagah."

<table>
<tr><td><u>No. and name</u></td><td><u>Status</u></td><td><u>Comment</u></td></tr>
</table>

		The weight of the evidence favors certainly two and probably three villages. Waterman ascribes 2 houses to rliiken-pets, to which may be added another 2 for tawchter. Across the river howego may also have had 4 houses.
24. rnr	C	Waterman says this town was being abandoned before the coming of the whites but it is shown on Kroeber's map and also on Randall's map of 1866. Hence it must have persisted for at least twenty years after the white invasion.
25. nagil	C	See no. 28.
26. ayol	C	See no. 28.
27. awpaw	P	See no. 28.
28. torah	P	Informants of Waterman recalled 4 houses at nagil, settled by the great-grandmother of Weitschpek Frank. The latter was a man of approximately forty years of age when Waterman saw him in 1909. Hence, allowing twenty-five years per generation and assuming that the ancestor was twenty-five years old when the place was founded, it must have been settled definitely prior to 1850.

Regarding ayol, which Kroeber shows (map, a standard town, Waterman says it was a "small settlement." He thinks the place was early abandoned and resettled more recently. However Merriam refers to it as a "village—opposite mouth of Ahpah Creek" and identifies it with the jehehak on Randall's map.

Merriam refers to awpaw as a "village on south bank Klamath at mouth of Ah Pah Creek, opposite and straight west of oyawsl (ayol)." He also says that torah was an "old village on west side of Klamath, close to nigehl, opposite mouth of Blue Creek." It is also on Randall's map.

No. and name	Status	Comment
		From the evidence of Randall and Merriam it appears probable that there were no less than four villages at this point on the river. Waterman gives 4 houses of nagil and 2 for ayol. The other two villages may be tentatively assigned 3 each.
29. srpr	C	At one time of some importance. Contained 3 houses "in memory of people now living and had been larger than that." Destroyed by flood in 1862.
30. tekta	C	Kroeber states that tekta had been occupied recently but did not seem to be an old site. This is directly contradicted by Waterman who calls it "an old town site." The name was frequently mentioned by his informants. Moreover he knew of a very old woman who was married from there as a girl and who "belongs" in tekta.
31. otsal	D	"A former village site," now destroyed. "The present Indians know nothing about a town here."
32. woxkero	C	See no. 34.
33. woxtek	C	See no. 34.
34. qootep	C	There is no question concerning the aboriginal existence of these towns. Confusion among modern informants has been due to population shifts caused by the flood of 1862, which damaged qootep.
35. pekwan	C	An "important place."
36. yoxtr	C	No question.
37. sregon	C	Waterman says: "Everyone agrees that it has not been there very long." Some informants said it was settled by people from woxtek or pekwan. But Waterman says: "... it may have been built before either of the other places." The town is on Randall's map and is mentioned in the 1852 census. Moreover Kroeber says that it "... enjoyed a reputation for belligerence and wealth." Its existence can therefore not be doubted.

No. and name	Status	Comment
38. kexkem	P	A site with house pits. The traces of habitation were "quite clear." But Waterman could get "no reference to the people." Kroeber considers. that it was inhabited only from time to time. However Merriam lists a village called leggoonaw which was "on south bank of Klamath between Mettah and Serragon." This appears to be the exact location of Waterman's kexkem and it may well have been the same village. Its existence is thus probable and 3 houses may be ascribed to it.
39. wererger	P	Merriam mentions this as a "village on north bank Klamath River, across from Mettah and a little above it." At this spot Waterman shows on his map no. 11 an "old village site" (his key no. 117). Hence the existence of the village is probable.
40. meta	C	No question.
41. keperor	P	Numerous house pits but informants never saw the houses. "The inhabitants all died at once and so the site has never been used since." A reasonable conclusion is that a village existed but that the people died of disease of epidemic character. (Cf. no. 13.)
42. nohtskum	C	A town with only house pits remaining but of undoubted existence.
43. weiqem	P	A site with 7 or 8 pits. Informants could not remember any houses. Some said it was a camp site but they had an elaborate legend to explain the house pits. The site is at the mouth of Roach Creek on the south bank of the river and hence a spot where one would normally expect a town to be located. Moreover the number of house pits is in excess of what would be anticipated for a mere camp site.

44. himel	C	This was a town, but the informants could barely remember the houses. Waterman could not determine why the inhabitants had disappeared. Kroeber mentions the village as one which may have been inhabited intermittently or temporarily and shows it thus on his map. However, he refers to it as a distinct town and lists it jointly with murek on It doubtless disappeared early as a separate entity.
45. murek	C	No question.
46. saa	C	No question.
47. kepel	C	No question.
48. waase	C	A "fairly large town." The people were rich.
49. merip	C	A small place with only one house name known. Its existence, however is confirmed by Merriam.
50. aukweya	P	See no. 53.
51. qenekpul	P	See no. 53.
52. tsetskwi	C	See no. 53.
53. qenek	C	Some question exists concerning these four villages. Kroeber nowhere mentions aukweya, but shows qenekpul and tsetskwi as temporary or briefly occupied towns and qenek as a permanent town. Waterman says that aukweya was a "settlement, three houses and a sweathouse." There had been no houses for many years and the pits were washed out. qenekpul was important mythologically and was said to have been built by an old Indian from turip but there is no record of house pits or early habitations. tsetskwi was a settlement with 3 houses and a sweathouse. In the youth of one informant there had been at least one family head living there, who was very old. Merriam lists all four sites as villages.

<u>*No. and name*</u>   <u>*Status*</u>   <u>*Comment*</u>

		There seems to be no serious question concerning the former existence of tsetskwi and qenek. It is highly probable that the other two sites were inhabited at the middle of the nineteenth century. Waterman in his list ascribes a total of 10 houses to the group, a reasonable figure
54. wahsek	C	No question.
55. weitspus	C	No question.
56. rlrgr	C	"... always a small place" but several of its families were rich. On Kroeber's map.
57. pekwutul	C	"... slightly larger than rlrgr" but had some wealthy citizens. On Kroeber's map.
58. loolego	C	Shown on Kroeber's map as a standard town. Waterman says that 30 years before his visit, i.e., in 1879, 2 pits and a sweathouse were to be seen there. loolego "... must at one time have been considerably larger for these people made up one of four parties who carried on the public spectacles in the deer skin ceremony at weitspus. They could not have done this had they not been rather numerous.... They were obviously influential people." This condition must have obtained long before 1879 when only house pits were known. The site was destroyed by mining in the 1880's.
59. aiqoo	C	Waterman says: "... at least two houses and a sweathouse stood here." Kroeber considers aiqoo as a subdivision of otsepor but Merriam lists it as a separate village, under the name Ikocho.
60. otsepor	C	In 1909 when Waterman saw it the village had merely three house pits. But an informant "... well remembers when several families ... lived here. They had fine large houses."
61. espaw	C	No question as to existence. Informants remember 4 houses but Waterman thinks that "in aboriginal times the number must have been much larger".

No. and name	Status	Comment
62. otmekwor	D	There are 5 house pits but Waterman thinks this is a true archaeological site, the inhabitants having moved across to oreqw several generations ago. On Kroeber's map as not a permanent settlement.
63. oreqw	C	No question.
64. oraw	D	Waterman, Kroeber, and Merriam all agree that this was a camp site.
65. sigwets	C	"... a suburb of oreqw. At least two houses and a sweathouse stood here and I think originally there may have been more." In view of Waterman's positive assertion the existence of the village may be admitted.
66. hrgwrw	C	"One informant said there were seven houses and two sweathouses."
67. tsahpekw	C	"Eleven house names were obtained."
68. tsotskwi	C	"An important Indian village stood here, but has not been inhabited since more than a generation ago.... One informant remembered having seen twelve houses and two sweathouses here."
69. paar	C	See no. 75.
70. osloqw	C	See no. 75.
71. kekem	P	See no. 75.
72. maats	C	See no. 75.
73. opyuweg	C	See no. 75.
74. pinpa	D	See no. 75.
75. oketo	P	These villages were located on Big Lagoon. The latter "... was a center of population. At least six inhabited sites were to be found about its shores...." At the same time Waterman admits that his notes were scanty and contradictory. "Undoubtedly the list of place names which I obtained in this locality could easily be expanded threefold...." "Enormous numbers of water birds still frequent the lagoon and must have been an important resource for the natives."

No. and name	*Status*	*Comment*

The villages of paar, osloqw, maats and opyuweg are shown on Kroeber's map as standard towns although kekem is mentioned as probably transitory and pinpa is not mentioned at all. Waterman states that paar was a town of considerable size. With respect to osloqw he says: "A very aged informant had never seen houses here but her predecessors had." This indicates an early and rapid disintegration of the village complex in the locality. The existence of both maats and opyuweg at the time of white settlement is conceded by both Waterman and Kroeber. Waterman thinks that pinpa was simply a suburb of opyuweg since he could obtain no house names here. oketo is given by Waterman as the name, in Yurok, of Big Lagoon. It is listed by Kroeber however as a village (both as oketo and chwaltaike, its Hupa name). Merriam says that oketo is the "... Polikla name for Nererner village at Big Lagoon." Its existence therefore is highly probable.

If Waterman is correct in his opinion that there were originally six villages around Big Lagoon, then all those mentioned, except pinpa, may be included. For the first five Waterman gives a total of 35 houses, or 7 houses per village. If the same ratio is used, 7 houses may be assigned to oketo, making in all 42.

76. olem	P	Waterman considers this a camp site but Merriam in his list of Yurok villages states it as "... Nererner name for their village at Patrick's Point." To assign 3 houses is probably adequate.
77. tsurai	C	No question.

<u>No. and name</u>	<u>Status</u>	<u>Comment</u>
78. srepor	C	. Some informants told Waterman that there were 4 houses and a sweathouse. On permanency of habitation he has no information. Kroeber on his map shows the site as a transitory village he mentions Little River "... at whose mouth stood the Yurok town of Metskwo (srepor)." Merriam also mentions Matskaw, a "village at mouth of Little River, on north side ..." Its aboriginal existence may therefore be taken as at least highly probable.

TABLE 2

Numbers of Houses

The figures in the first column are for village sites as listed in table 1. Sources: R, Randall's map; 1. Waterman's list (1920. p. 206); t. Waterman's text (1920); M. Merriam's village lists; p, an estimate.

<u>No.</u>	<u>Source</u>	<u>House Count</u>	<u>Kroeber, "modern memories"</u>	<u>Kroeber, 1852 census</u>
1	1	7		
2	t	4		
3	1	25	} 23+	} 22+
4	1	9		
5	tp	3		
6	tp	3		
7	Mp	3		
8	Mp	3		
12	1	4		
13	1	4	9	6
14	1	3	2	2
15	Mp	8		
17	Mp	3		
18	1	5	5	2
19	t	8	8+	14
20	Rp	3		

No.	Source	House Count	Kroeber, "modern memories"	Kroeber, 1852 census
21	lp	4		
22	Rp	4		
24	l	3		
25	t	4		
26	t	2		
27	Mp	3		
28	Mp	3		
29	l	3	3	4
30	tp	3		
32	l	4	} 13	} 7
33	l	13		
34	l	22	18	24
35	l	24	17+	20
36	l	4	4	3
37	l	5	6	7
38	Mp	3		
39	Mp	3		
40	l	6	7	6
41	tp	5		
42	l	3	4	4
43	tp	6		
44	l	4	} 21	} 14
45	l	11		
45	l	8	} 14	} 6
47	l	4		
48	l	6		
49	l	5		
50	l	3		
51	l	1		
52	l	2		
53	l	4		
54	l	6		

No.	Source	House Count	Kroeber, "modern memories"	Kroeber, 1852 census
55	l	17		
56	l	6		
57	l	5		
58	l	4		
59	l	2		
60	l	3		
61	l	7		
63	l	7		
65	t	2		
66	l	5		
67	l	10		
68	l	5		
69	tp	5		
70	tp	3		
71	t	4		
72	l	5		
73	l	18		
75	Mp	7		
76	Mp	3		
77	l	14		
78	t	4		

THE WIYOT

There are three primary ethnographic sources for the population of the Wiyot. The first is the extensive monograph by Loud (1918), the second a short paper by Nomland and Kroeber (1936), and the third the village lists of Merriam.

Loud based his data on interviews with numerous informants together with a rather cursory visual inspection of the region. He shows nearly two hundred sites of all kinds on his map and differentiates by means of conventional symbols between what he calls "archaeological" and "modern village" sites. By the latter he means settlements which were occupied at approximately the time of the American invasion of 1850. In his text he discusses descriptively a few of the more important of the "modern village" sites but for most of the smaller places he furnishes no information other than inclusion on his map. His coverage is fairly good for the valley of the Mad River and for Humboldt Bay but his treatment of the valley of the Eel River is nearly worthless. Recognizing this deficiency in Loud's data, Nomland and Kroeber secured the services of an informant who was born in 1860 in this area and had lived there all his life. They were thus able to obtain a very complete list of sites, together with a fairly accurate house count for each of them. This list is therefore as reliable as we shall ever be able to get and, unless we wish to discard this type of information completely, we must accept it as essentially correct.

For the Mad River and Humboldt Bay areas the recently acquired village lists of Merriam form an admirable supplement to Loud's compilation. Merriam went over the ground personally and checked carefully Loud's sites. He was thus able to clarify many of the obscurities in the data furnished by the earlier investigator. Where points of discrepancy arise between the two authors therefore, more reliance may be placed upon Merriam.

The family number is taken by Kroeber (1925. p. 116) as the same as for the Yurok, i.e., 7.5. Loud obtained estimates for both house number and population for three villages. Site 45 gave 13.5 persons per house, site 67 gave 9, and site 112 gave 5. The average is slightly over 9, a figure which has no further significance than to indicate that the Yurok value of 7.5 may be applied safely to the Wiyot.

With respect to Kroeber's principle of a one-third reduction in the number of houses the same considerations apply as with the Yurok data. There is nothing to indicate in the work of either Loud or Nomland and Kroeber that informants were not thinking in terms of inhabited houses rather than total deserted houses or house pits. Indeed we have in Loud's text three specific instances (nos. 7, 67, and Y) where the informant not only stated that the houses were occupied in the early days but also gave the names of the persons living in all of them. It is difficult to reconcile a one-third reduction with such data.

In table 3 (pp. 94-96, herein) are given a few notes, gleaned mainly from Loud and supplemented from Merriam's list, which are of interest in determining the existence and population of certain villages. All villages are included the existence of which in approximately 1850 Loud regards as reasonably certain. To these are added several of Loud's doubtful sites, the validity of which has been confirmed by Merriam, plus five villages missed by Loud but discovered by Merriam. The house counts for those towns confirmed or discovered by Merriam have had to be estimated. The number has been taken rather uniformly as 2 or 3 in order to maintain as conservative a standard as possible. For 22 of the larger and better known sites Loud's informants gave an average of 6.5 houses. Hence an average of 3 for those whose names and locations only were known seems in no way excessive.

In table 4 (herein) are shown the best estimates for the Mad River and Humboldt Bay areas from Loud and Merriam and for the Eel River valley from Nomland and Kroeber. The total is 440. At 7.5 persons per house this means a population of 3,300 inhabitants for the Wiyot. The corresponding figure given by Kroeber in the Handbook is "perhaps 800 or not over 1,000." Loud states on page 302: "If asked to give an extreme figure for the native population ... the writer would say 1,500, and consider any higher figure pure folly." The present writer, however, stands by the figure of approximately 3,300, insofar as the estimate is based on ethnographic material.

It was suggested in connection with the Yurok that this tribe was already undergoing some reduction in population at the time of the first entry of Americans en masse in 1850 and that the best memory of informants in the decade 1900-1910 could not give us the truly aboriginal picture. For the Wiyot the evidence is still more impressive. None of Loud's white informants could go back of 1850 and one gets the impression that his Indian informants could do little better. John Sherman, the informant of Nomland and Kroeber, was born in 1860, subsequent to ten years of massacre and disintegration of native society. This state of affairs is reflected in many statements in Loud's text. (See also table 3, pp. 94-96, herein.) For instance several strikingly large and recent graveyards are mentioned, a statement which can refer only to the period of 1850 or immediately before. Site 22, according to tradition, had once possessed a large population, and site 23 was said to have been a "regular rancheria" one hundred years previously (that is, previous to 1918). Nevertheless the population of these towns could not be included in the present estimate because no informant living in this century could remember houses there. Site 68 had been declining prior to 1850, the inhabitants either dying or moving elsewhere. The tremendous destruction of population *after* 1850 is everywhere evident in Loud's account and it is not too much to suppose that the confusion of the period is reflected in too *low* values given by modern informants. If this is true, then it is quite possible that the estimate given here of 3,300 Wiyot is actually considerably lower than the true aboriginal population, rather than higher.

WIYOT ... 3,300

TABLE 3

Wiyot Sites listed by Loud (1918)

Notes and comment with respect to some of Loud's sites. Page numbers unless otherwise specified refer to Loud (1918). The notation "Merriam" indicates that the site was checked and accepted by Merriam, who included it in his village list of the Wiyot. The letter A signifies that Merriam had obtained an Athapascan name for the site, thus confirming its existence as an entity known to the neighboring tribes in pre-American times.

Loud's Sites	*Comment*
Site 3	Merriam
Site 4	Merriam (A)
Site 5	Merriam (A)
Site 6	Merriam (A)
Site 7	There were 11 houses, all occupied, the names of the families known to Loud's informant.
Site 8	Merriam

<table>
<tr><td><u>Loud's Sites</u></td><td><u>Comment</u></td></tr>
</table>

Sites H, I, J, 9	These are located in the former Big Bend of the Mad River. A pioneer told Loud that there had once been 20 houses in the area. Another informant said that site I had been "one of the largest villages" and "... had a large graveyard." Site 9 was said by Curtis (Nomland and Kroeber, p. 44) to have had 5 houses. Loud's informant gave it 5 or 6. Hence the estimate of the pioneer appears quite reasonable. Merriam lists all four sites with their Wiyot and Athapascan names.
Sites D through G K through X AA through AK	These sites extend along Mad River and around the shores of Blue Lake. Loud gives no specific data concerning them and some are individually doubtful. However, Loud says that the houses were scattered along both banks of the river and the shores of the lake. "That is, about every mile there was an Indian house or two." Although Loud was not very accurate in the location of the sites, it is quite probable that scattered homes existed in at least the ratio of one dwelling to each site mentioned. Hence it is reasonable to ascribe a minimum of at least one house per site. This would yield a total of 29 houses.
	Loud's data were checked and revised by Merriam, who appears to have done a more careful piece of work on this area than Loud. Merriam confirms and gives Wiyot and Athapascan names for Loud's villages E, G, K, L, M, N, O, P, Q, R, S, T, U, V, W, X, AA, AB, AC, and AG, or 20 villages in all. The minimum number of houses which can be ascribed to a "village" is 2. On the other hand several of the 20 sites must have contained more than the minimum and therefore it would be legitimate to set the average at 3. This would mean a total of 60 houses for the entire area covered by these villages.
Site Y	The site had 4 houses, all occupied, the names of the occupants known to Loud's informant. Merriam (A).
Site Z	This town was destroyed by the Chilula just prior to 1850. The whites found 30 to 40 fresh graves. Merriam says it was the "chief village in vicinity of Blue Lake at time of Chilula attack."

Loud's Sites	Comment
Site 14	Stated by Loud to be a camping place but called a village by Merriam. Status doubtful.
Site 17	Merriam.
Site 19	Merriam.
Site 22	"... according to tradition once had a large population." Loud thinks it was uninhabited by 1850 but Merriam lists it as a village. Estimate 4 houses.
Site 23	"... said to be a regular rancheria one hundred years ago." Nomland and Kroeber say it has been uninhabited in modern times and Merriam considers it an archaeological site.
Site 31	A summer camp according to Loud but a village according to Merriam. Allow 2 houses.
Site 33	"This village was referred to as a 'regular rancheria' when the whites first came, a statement which is confirmed by the number of skeletons that have been found here with white man's articles buried with them." Listed by Merriam. Estimate 8 houses.
Site 34	Loud found no houses and only 2 house pits. However in 1890 there were 20 graves which were visited by relatives. Listed by Merriam. Estimate 4 houses.
Site 36	Stated by Merriam to be an archaeological site.
Site 39	Merriam. Estimate 2 houses.
Site AL	According to an informant there were several houses in 1856 with one occupied. Listed by Merriam. Estimate 4 houses.
Site 45	According to an informant there were 2 houses and 25 to 30 inhabitants in 1852. Deserted in 1860.
Site 48	Merriam. Estimate 2 houses.
Site 58	The site was known to pioneers, who said it had 8 to 10 houses in 1858. Listed by Merriam. Estimate 9 houses.
Site 65	There were three to four houses in 1852. The inhabitants were driven out shortly afterward. Listed by Merriam. Estimate 3.5 houses.

Loud's Sites	Comment
Site 67	An informant said there were 9 houses once, all occupied, the names of the persons being known to him. Robert Gunther told Loud that in 1860 there were 6 houses left with 50 to 60 persons. "Estimates of population ... in 1850 have been placed much higher, but after the introduction of certain diseases by the whites, the population decreased somewhat." Estimate 9 houses.
Site 68	The village had been declining prior to 1850. At the time the population was one-third that of site 67. The last family moved in 1857 when a white man took up the land. Estimate 3 houses.
Site 69	Merriam. Estimate 3 houses.
Site 73	There were 8 to 10 plank houses here in 1851. Listed by Merriam. Estimate 9 houses.
Site 77	White informants say there were not more than half-a-dozen houses, although an Indian says many people used to live here. Listed by Merriam. Estimate 6 houses.
Site 79	Nomland and Kroeber say this was one of the two largest Wiyot towns, hence there were at least 10 houses. It was destroyed in 1850 by white settlement.
Site 80	Merriam. Estimate 3 houses.
Site 83	Merriam. Estimate 3 houses.
Site 84	Merriam. Estimate 3 houses.
Site 86	"... a permanent village." Listed by Merriam. Estimate 3 houses.
Site 88	Merriam. Estimate 3 houses.
Site 90	Merriam. Estimate 3 houses.
Site 91	A camping place, according to Loud, but a village on Merriam's lists. Allow 2 houses.
Site AM	Merriam. Estimate 3 houses.
Site 92	Merriam. Estimate 3 houses.
Site 93	Merriam. Estimate 3 houses.
Site 98	Merriam. Estimate 3 houses.
Site 100	Merriam. Estimate 3 houses.

Loud's Sites	*Comment*
Site 102	Loud says camping place, Merriam village. Allow 2 houses.
Site 104	Shown as archaeological site on Loud's map but given by Merriam as a village. Allow 2 houses.
Site 109	Merriam. Estimate 3 houses.
Site 112	The village had 10 houses and at least 51 inhabitants before the massacre of 1860.
Other sites	In addition to the above sites found by Loud there are five listed by name by Merriam. These should be included and assigned an average of 3 houses each. The total then would be 15.

TABLE 4

Wiyot Settlements

Mad River and Humboldt Bay

Wiyot settlements according to Loud, Merriam, and Nomland and Kroeber, covering the Mad River and Humboldt Bay. The key designations are those given by Loud. The house counts are from Loud with the exception of sites B and C which are from Nomland and Kroeber and of several sites from Merriam for which I have made my own estimates (indicated by the letters *Mp.*). In all instances where a range is given by informants (e.g., 2-4 houses) the mean is placed in the table.

Loud's no.	*House count*	
3	3	Mp
4 and 5	12.5	
6	3	Mp
7	11	
8	3	Mp
H, I, J, 9	20	
D-G		
K-X	60	Mp
AA-AK		
A	8	
B	4	

Loud's no.	House count	
C	5.5	
Y	4	
Z	12	
17	4.5	
19	3	Mp
22	4	Mp
31	2	Mp
33	8	Mp
34	4	Mp
39	2	Mp
45	2	
AL	4	Mp
48	2	Mp
58	9	
65	3.5	
67	9	
68	3	
69	3	Mp
73	9	
77	6	
79	10	
80	3	Mp
83	3	Mp
84	3	Mp
86	3	Mp
88	3	Mp
90	3	Mp
91	2	Mp
AM	3	Mp
92	3	Mp
93	3	Mp
98	3	Mp
100	3	Mp

Loud's no.	_House count_	
102	2	Mp
104	2	Mp
109	3	Mp
112	10	
Others	15	Mp
Total	299	

Eel River

Wiyot settlements on the Eel River as given to Nomland and Kroeber by the informant John Sherman. The villages are numbered consecutively from the list on pages 40 to 42 of their paper (1936). The list here is cut off at village no. 32, which Kroeber, following Powers, puts as the limit of the Wiyot. The presence of the Wiyot racial group above this point is controversial. For numerous towns the informant uses the non-specific terms "few," "many," etc. These expressions have been transformed arbitrarily, but I think conservatively, into numerical form as follows: Few = 2; several = 4; many = 8; large = 10.

Serial No.	_Sherman's estimate of house count_	_Final estimate_
1.	few	2
2.	few	2
3.	2-3	2.5
4.	2-3	2.5
5.	5-10	7.5
6.	5-10	7.5
7.	4-5	4.5
8.	1-2	1.5
9.	1-2	1.5
10.	10 plus	10
11.	5-6	5.5
12.	several	4
13.	several	4
14.	1-2	1.5
15.	1-2	1.5

Serial No.	Sherman's estimate of house count	Final estimate
16.	5-10	7.5
17.	few	2
18.	0	0
19.	5-10	7.5
20.	0	0
21.	large "20"	10
22.	several	4
23.	many	8
24.	many	8
25.	several	4
26.	several	4
27.	several	4
28.	several	4
29.	no statement	
30.	many	8
31.	inhabited	2
32.	many	8
Total		139

THE KAROK

The village distribution of the Karok was treated briefly by Kroeber in the Handbook, and far more exhaustively in a later paper (1936). For the latter he secured the services of two good informants, a very elderly Indian man named Ned and a woman, Mary Jacops, with whom he examined the area carefully. The list set forth of his publication must be regarded as definitive. It is true that Merriam has a very complete list of Karok villages but his names vary linguistically from those of Kroeber to such an extent that, save in a few instances, it is extremely difficult to reconcile them. However, since Merriam's total is 115 for the same territory where Kroeber finds 108 and since Merriam does not give house counts the Kroeber list may be used exclusively.

Ned gave house counts but Mrs. Jacops did not. Kroeber amplified wherever possible with data from Curtis (cited by Kroeber, p. 30, as The North American Indian, 13:222). Ned's counts were very cautious since he distinguished frequently between the number of houses he had seen at a given site and the number he had heard were there. On the basis of such distinctions Kroeber reduces the total count by a factor of one-sixth. He states:

> Among the Yurok ... two occupied houses may be reckoned
> for each three house sites recognized when full detailed data
> are at hand. They are obviously not detailed for the Karok.

I must take issue with two points. With the Karok the counts were not based upon house sites recognized but on the memory of *inhabited houses* by informants. Hence the house site or pit theory cannot apply. In the second place, a reasonably thorough examination of the *published* material on the Yurok, Wiyot, and the Karok shows that the data for the Karok presented by Kroeber represents the fullest detail of all with respect to the number of houses.

Apropos of the same question it is of interest to point out the house counts given by Ned for the fifteen villages also provided with counts by Curtis for 1860. Kroeber has tabulated these himself and shows that, despite variation in individual detail, the total for Ned is 60 and that for Curtis is

57-60. The identity is remarkable. Commenting on this situation, Kroeber makes the following very significant statement (p. 35. fn.):

> It is apparent that, for any particular settlement, no precise figure, even by a good informant, is very reliable unless based on an enumeration of named houses. But for a larger series of settlements the particular variations, resulting from changes of residence or difference of times referred to, tend to cancel each other out and to yield *comparable and fairly reliable totals.*

(Emphasis mine.) The present writer, consequently, can see no necessity for a gross reduction of one-sixth of the computed population.

Kroeber's list shows 108 towns plus 10 mentioned by Curtis as being in Karok territory on the Salmon River. The first 84 villages were covered by Ned, who gave house counts for 61 of them. Using wherever possible the houses actually seen, not merely heard of, by Ned we get a total of 248. This is a little smaller than Kroeber's total for the same sites of 254. In this group of 84 villages 9 have counts from Curtis but not from Ned, with a total of 24 houses. By Kroeber's own showing Curtis' counts are as reliable in the aggregate as those of Ned. Sites 85 to 108 are derived only from Mrs. Jacops who did not give counts. Kroeber proposes to reduce these to 15 settlements and assign an average value of 4 houses per village. This seems entirely reasonable, and gives us 60 houses. We may now add the 10 villages on the Salmon River cited from Curtis by Kroeber and, to be conservative, assign an average count of 3 houses each. The total of all Karok houses then becomes 362. At the customary 7.5 persons per house the population of the Karok is 2,715. or with sufficient accuracy, 2,700.

KAROK ... 2,700

THE HUPA

There are four sources of consequence for the Hupa population. The first is the discussion to be found the Handbook by Kroeber, which includes a census furnished to the government by the Yurok in 1851. The second is a monograph published by Goddard (1903). The third is a particularly exhaustive village list compiled by Merriam. The fourth is a map drawn by Gibbs in 1852, photostatic copies of which are to be found in the Merriam collection.

The towns of the Hupa fall naturally into two subdivisions, the first comprising those in Hupa Valley proper and the second those above the valley which extended along the main Trinity River and its South Fork. The first included 12 villages which are mentioned by name by Goddard and are shown on his map. For most of them he indicates houses by dots and solid squares which can easily be counted. Kroeber lists the same 12 towns and all but one of them appear on Merriam's list. (These are numbered 1-12 in table 5. p. 100, herein.) Village no. 2, Dakis-hankut, is omitted by Merriam but is shown with houses by Goddard. Village no. 8, Totltsasding, is stated by Kroeber to have been "unoccupied in 1850." Goddard however merely says that it had been deserted for a long time. On the other hand it had been sufficiently well known to the Yurok for them to have a name for it, and Merriam does not question its existence. These two villages may therefore be retained in the list.

With regard to the second group Kroeber gives two villages (nos. 13 and 14) as "permanent settlements." Above these come five towns (nos. 15 to 19 inclusive) lying on the main Trinity River, which are mentioned by name by Kroeber. Although they are mentioned "in early sources" as being in the area Kroeber nevertheless does not think they should be added to his list. However, they are cited by Merriam, for the same area, and three of them are shown with house counts on Gibbs's map. Their existence seems therefore to be assured. They are probably the "5 other villages in and above Hupa Valley, not positively identified" which are cited in the Yurok list by Kroeber

No. 20, Tjelding, is given by Kroeber as certain and is included by Merriam. The remaining villages, although not specifically mentioned by Kroeber or Goddard, are given in his list by Merriam with the explicit statement that "these were permanent villages. There were also several camps along the south side of Trinity." Since Merriam is the only investigator who has made a thorough examination of this area, his work must be accepted.

With respect to house counts it is interesting to compare the six villages in Hupa Valley which occur, on the one hand, on the Yurok list of Kroeber or on the Gibbs map and, on the other hand, on Goddard's map. The former give a total count for these towns of 82 houses, whereas Goddard shows 78. The Yurok census and Gibbs's map were formulated in 1851 and 1852 immediately after the advent of the whites. Goddard presumably derived his data from informants in or about the year 1900. From the two sets of figures it is clear that Goddard's cannot be too high and therefore those he gives for villages not covered by the earlier sources must be reasonably reliable. Goddard's total for 11 sites is 128, or an average of 11.6 houses per settlement. In default of other information this value, rounded off to 11, may be applied to no. 8.

Passing to the second group, we find that the five villages above Hupa Valley on the main Trinity River are shown on the 1851 census list as having 23 houses. The map by Gibbs assigns house counts to three of these, nos. 15, 16, and 19 with 4, 3, and 6 houses respectively. The average from the census is 4.6 houses per village and that from Gibbs is 4.3. We may accept from these data the value 4.5 as representing the mean house count for villages outside Hupa Valley proper. This is notably lower than the mean for the valley itself but is consistent with the poorer, more remote terrain.

Using Goddard's counts and the 1851 census where possible and supplementing by the estimate given above for the other villages we get a total of 198 houses for the Hupa. At 7.5 persons per house the population would have been 1,485. This is considerably above Kroeber's "barely 1.000"

A further question presents itself at this point. Should we accept without reservation the Yurok value of 7.5 inhabitants per house? Two lines of evidence become pertinent here. Goddard in describing Hupa society makes the following statements:

> A typical family consisted of the man and his sons, the wife or wives of the man, the unmarried or half-married daughters, the wives of the sons, and the grandchildren. To these may be added unmarried or widowed brothers or sisters of the man and his wife.... All the children born in the *same house* called each other brothers and sisters, whether they were children of the same parents or not.

(Emphasis mine.) To this Kroeber adds (p. 132): "The ultimate basis of this life is obviously blood kinship, but the *immediately controlling factor is the association of common residence; in a word, the house.*" Now the social family in the usual monogamous tribe included the father, mother, children, and occasional close relatives. This was the underlying assumption of Kroeber's estimate of 7.5 persons as the social family among the Yurok. Here, very clearly, the social family was far more extensive, perhaps in occasional instances as much as double the Yurok value. At any rate the value 7.5 seems definitely too low.

Another approach is through the data furnished by Kroeber of the Handbook. Here he shows a population census taken from seven villages in the year 1870 (the last item "sawmill" may be deleted as impossible to place). The total is 601 persons. Goddard's data show for these same seven villages a house count of 92 for the years centering around 1850. The direct average number of persons per house would be 6.53. Meanwhile Kroeber points out the disparity between the sexes: 232 males and 359 females. This he attributes to warfare alone, a dubious conclusion. Regardless of cause, however, we may calculate that in the absence of this male mortality and with a normal sex ratio of approximately unity the population would have been twice the female number or 718. The average number per house under such conditions would then have been 7.80.

It must be borne in mind that the population count is of 1870 and the house count is of 1850 or earlier. Although Kroeber feels that there was no population decline, apart from the effect of warfare on the males just mentioned, I cannot agree with him. In the face of the overwhelming evidence for a tremendous decline subsequent to 1850 on the part of the Indian population throughout all California it is impossible to concede complete immunity to any one tribe no matter how well protected it might have been. Consequently, we must allow for a reduction from 1850 to 1870 even on the part of the females. It is impracticable to set any sure figure on the decline but a value of 20 per cent would be very conservative, particularly in comparison with all the northwestern tribes. This would mean a population for the seven villages of 879, or say 900 in 1850. On this basis the number of persons per house becomes 9.78.

I think therefore we are justified in ascribing 10 persons to each Hupa house. If so the population would have been 1,980, or approximately 2,000. It is entirely possible that even this is too conservative an estimate.

HUPA ... 2,000

TABLE 5

Hupa Villages

According to Kroeber (K), Goddard (Go), Gibbs (Gi), and Merriam (M). The numbering is purely arbitrary and is based on Kroeber's list. The house counts are from Goddard's map, the Yurok census of 1851 as cited by Kroeber, and the 1852 map of Gibbs.

No. and Name	Houses from 1851 census	Houses from Goddard's map	Houses from Gibb's map	Houses by estimate
1. Honsading: K, M, Go, Gi	9	11	9	
2. Dakis-hankut: K, Go		7		
3. Kinchuwikut: K, M, Go		8		
4. Cheindekotding: K, M, Go		12		
5. Miskut: K, M, Go, Gi	6	11	6	
6. Takimitlding: K, M, Go, Gi	20	14	20	
7. Tsewenalding: K, M, Go, Gi	10	6	10	
8. Totltsasding: K, M, Go				8
9. Medilding: K, M, Go, Gi	28	23	28	
10. Djishtangading: K, M, Go, Gi		13	9	
11. Howunkut: K, M, Go		14		

No. and Name	Houses from 1851 census	Houses from Goddard's map	Houses from Gibb's map	Houses by estimate
12. Haslinding: K, M, Go		9		
13. Kachwunding: K				4.5
14. Mingkutme: K				4.5
15. Sehachpeya: K, Gi, M			4	
16. Waugullewatl: K, Gi, M			3	
17. Ahelta: K, M	23			
18. Sokeakeit: K, M				
19. Tashuanta: K, M, Gi			6	
20. Tjelding: K, M	3			
21. Tiltswetchaki: M				4.5
22. Chilchtaltung: M				4.5
23. Ostantung: M				4.5
24. Hlitchchoochtung: M				4.5
25. Klokumne: K, M				4.5
26. Tahchoochtung: M				4.5

THE TOLOWA

Apart from the discussion by Kroeber in the Handbook there have been two published attempts to enumerate the villages of the Tolowa. One of these was by Waterman (1925) and the other by Drucker (1937). Of all these the treatment by Drucker is the most complete since he had the advantage of a knowledge of the earlier work. Although he may have missed settlements in the interior, for present purposes we must accept his list as a working basis.

Drucker mentions 23 villages, all located on the coast or along the lower reaches of the Smith River. Kroeber gives 10 sites from which he computes the population, at the Yurok rate of 45 inhabitants per village, as 450. Waterman gives 14 places, which, at the same rate, would yield 630. Drucker has house counts for 13 of his villages, with a total of 88 houses or 6.76 houses per village. At the Yurok count of 7.5 persons per house, which Kroeber says applies to the Tolowa, the average population per village would be 51. Kroeber's estimate of 45 is thus quite close. There is no good reason to suppose, in view of the lack of any good evidence to the contrary that the other 10 villages of Drucker were smaller than those for which he gave house counts. Thus we may add 68 houses, making a total of 156 and a population of 1,186. Kroeber would of course reduce by one-third but the reasons for so doing are no more compelling with this than with any other tribe.

Drucker states that his house counts are as of 40 to 50 years ago. This means, first, that the houses were described to him by informants as known to them in their youth to be inhabited (hence no reduction necessary) and, second, that the counts represent the situation during the period of 1885 to 1895.

Now the counts published for all the tribes hitherto considered were based upon the conditions obtaining at approximately 1850, 35 to 45 years earlier. In other words, Drucker's figures cannot in any sense represent the aboriginal state, for there must have been a marked decline in population and in number of houses among the Tolowa between 1850 and 1890. The implication is, startling as it may seem, that the population estimate given above is much too low.

Some idea of what may have happened can be secured by a brief reconsideration of Waterman's Yurok data. It will be remembered that Waterman shows detailed maps of 19 villages, including not only houses once standing but also houses standing and inhabited when he saw them in 1909. The ratio of the former to the latter is 189 to 38. There were of course many more houses standing in 1890 than in 1909, although the population did not decline materially during these particular twenty years. Hence the ratio found by Waterman for the Yurok cannot be applied directly to the Tolowa. Nevertheless it is reasonable to assume that a count made among the Yurok in 1890 would have shown that not more than half as many houses were being inhabited then as had been in 1850. If so, Drucker's total of 156 might be doubled, giving 312 and a population of 2,372. Such an estimate may appear totally at variance with the other known facts pertaining to the tribe but I am inclined to adhere to it.

Further support for such a view comes from consideration of relative population decline since 1850. of the Handbook Kroeber cites the federal census of 1910 as showing 668 persons for the Yurok and on page 130 over 600 for the Hupa. He thinks that the Hupa were less numerous than the Karok and the latter less numerous than the Yurok. With respect to the Karok he says "It is also clear that the proportional loss of the Karok in the past 65 years has been relatively mild, possibly not exceeding one half." In another connection he discusses at some length the reasons why the Hupa suffered less than many other tribes—primarily because of their protected position and the lack of mining in their area. Now the Wiyot in 1910 had 150 people and the Tolowa 120. If their loss had been of the order of one half, as Kroeber feels is the case with the Yurok, Karok, and Hupa, then the population of the Wiyot in 1850 would have been in the vicinity of 300 and the Tolowa 240. Actually, in his original estimates Kroeber did set the figures for these tribes not much higher: 800 for the Wiyot and 450 for the Tolowa. Kroeber thus defeats his own argument with respect to the small decline and protected position of the Karok and Hupa. For the position of the Wiyot and the Tolowa were the most exposed to white influence of any of the Northwestern tribes. They were located on the fertile, commercial, and well settled coast. Many types of evidence point to their early and rapid disintegration and almost extinction. They should have suffered the worst losses and did. Hence it is not as far fetched as it might seem at first sight to ascribe to the Tolowa a population in 1850 of nearly 2,400.

TOLOWA ... 2,400

THE ATHAPASCANS

THE CHILULA

With the Chilula we encounter the first of the small Athapascan tribes of Northwestern California. Their villages have been studied intensively by Goddard (1910), who lists 18 but gives no house counts. 1Merriam, who re-examined Goddard's report likewise finds 18 sure villages plus 21 summer camps and 2 places of indeterminate character.

Merriam deviated from Kroeber very widely in his tribal names for the Athapascan groups. It is probably preferable to retain Kroeber's terminology without prejudice to Merriam simply because Kroeber's names are at the present time much the more widely accepted and used. Merriam's material pertaining to the Chilula is to be found in his manuscript entitled "Geographic Arrangement of Hwilkut Camps and Villages." He thus includes the Chilula among the Whilkut.

The closest approach to a house count is reported by Kroeber (1925, p. 138) who states that six of the identified settlements showed 17, 7, 4, 2, 4, and 8 house pits respectively. This is an average of 7. Kroeber considers that the customary one-third reduction should apply and in this instance with considerable justification, since there were no living informants and the villages had not been inhabited since the 1850's. However, the careful study of the Yurok by Waterman demonstrated that the apparent ratio of contemporary house pits to former known inhabited houses was approximately 10 to 9 rather than 3 to 2. It is hence legitimate to reduce the average value of houses per village for the Chilula from 7 to 6. With 18 sites this means 108 homes. Applying the Yurok value of 7.5 persons per house instead of the probable Hupa value of 10. we get a population of 810 persons. This is somewhat greater than Kroeber's estimate of 500 to 600.

Chilula ... 800

1Since completion of this manuscript, Mr. Martin R. Baumhoff of the Department of Anthropology has discovered village lists filed many years ago by Pliny E. Goddard, which cover Athapascan territory in addition to that held by the Wailaki. Mr. Baumhoff is now analyzing the new data and his results will probably necessitate an upward revision of the population figures given here.

THE MATTOLE

That portion of the Mattole living on Bear River have been studied by Nomland (1938) through information supplied by a single very old informant. The house and family relationships appear to resemble those found among the Wiyot directly to the north, although no numerical data of any kind are given. The data hitherto presented have yielded as average number of houses per village, 6.0 for the Yurok. 4.5 for the Wiyot, 6.8 for the Tolowa, and 6.0 for the Chilula. The mean of these averages is 5.8, or let us say in round numbers 6, a value which seems reasonable for those Athapascan tribes for which there are no direct counts. The Yurok family number of 7.5 also appears applicable.

Merriam in his list entitled "Nekanne Tribe and Villages" mentions only three villages on Bear River but Nomland (1938) in her more careful examination of the territory found 8. Hence the population of this group may be set at 360.

Apart from Bear River the Mattole territory included the drainages of Davis Creek and the Mattole River, together with the west bank of the Eel River for a short distance above the Wiyot. Davis Creek is much smaller than Bear Creek and probably was sparsely settled. Nevertheless Nomland's informant mentioned individuals who were from Davis Creek and hence it must be assumed that there was at least one and very likely as many as two villages there. The Mattole River was larger than Bear River and has been well covered by Merriam in his list entitled "Bettol or Pettol (Mattol) Tribe and Villages." He cites 10 named villages. In addition, he includes the Kooske, who he says were a "very large band and village ('hundreds of people') formerly on Koosky (or Cooskie) Creek on or near the coast 2-1/2 or 3 miles southeast of Punta Gorda lighthouse." He also cites two indentures for Indians of this tribe which he found in the Eureka court house.

The 2 villages on Davis Creek and the 10 on Mattole River would yield 540 persons. If we accept Merriam's description of the Kooske tribe, we may add another 300. The total for the Mattole would then be a population of 1,200.

Mattole ... 1,200

THE WHILKUT

For information on the Whilkut we are indebted to Merriam for the only village list extant. He covers the tribe, together with the Chilula, in his list entitled "Geographic Arrangement of Hwilkut Camps and Villages," revised, according to a pencil notation of the title sheet, in 1939.

Merriam gives 15 villages for the Hoechkienok or "Upper Redwood" tribe, 3 for the Kotinet or "Blue Lake and North Fork Mad River" tribe and 15 for the Mawenok, who lived "on Mad River from opposite Korbel up to the ranch of John Ahlgren about 21 miles in air line." The Chilula and Mattole were credited with 45 persons per village. The habitat of the Whilkut lies on smaller streams and is generally less favorable than that of the Chilula or the Mattole. Hence the number may be reduced to 40 per village. The total is then 1,320.

Whilkut ... 1,300

THE KATO

There are only two usable ethnographic sources of information concerning villages among the Kato. The first is the rather casual treatment given the group by Barrett (1908) in his monograph on the Pomo. He lists 17 villages as having existed in the area comprising the modern stretch running from Laytonville to Branscomb and a few miles north and south thereof. No village sizes and no discussion of community organization. Merriam in his list "Kahto Tribe and Villages" mentions the 17 villages of Barrett and adds 3 others derived from his own informants, making a total of 20.

Since there is no explicit information regarding village size, we may adopt the value used for the Whilkut, *i.e.*, 40 persons per village. This would mean a population of 800.

Barrett and Merriam, however, give data only for the southernmost part of the Kato range, including an area of approximately 150 square miles. The remainder of the Kato territory extended some distance along the upper waters of the South Fork of the Eel River and its area may be reckoned as 100 square miles or 40 per cent of the entire Kato territory. On the other hand, living conditions were not as good in this portion of the range and the density was probably less than in the vicinity of Laytonville and Branscomb. Hence we may add 300 persons (rather than the full 40 per cent) and consider the total as 1,100.

With the Kato we arrive at an area where it becomes possible to utilize historical and documentary, as well as ethnographic, sources of information. For the period 1850-1856 there are three accounts left us by white men who were direct observers, as distinguished from data supplied from memory to modern white men by Indian informants. With respect to the region north of San Francisco Bay these observations by Americans must be regarded as supplementary to the basic ethnographic material derived from Indians.

Nevertheless they are of considerable value in confirming, negating, or modifying the ethnographic data.

Two primary sources are pertinent here. The first is the expedition of Colonel Redick M'Kee, one of the three "commissioners" sent out in 1851 to negotiate treaties with the California Indians. M'Kee went first to Clear Lake, then up the Russian River, over to the Eel River watershed, down to Humboldt Bay, and eventually up the Klamath and Trinity rivers. Two records of this expedition were kept. The first, and far better known, is the Journal of George Gibbs, which was later published by Henry R. Schoolcraft (1860). The other is the Minutes of the expedition, written by John M'Kee, a relative of the Colonel. These Minutes, together with considerable correspondence, were published in Senate Executive Document No. 4, 33rd Congress, Special Session (1853).

The second source is a report written by Major H. P. Heintzelman at the request of Indian Agent Henley, in 1855. Major Heintzelman (1855) made a survey of the tribes of Sonoma and Mendocino counties which might be placed upon a reservation at the mouth of the Noyo River. He interviewed numerous headmen, or chiefs, of community units and reported on the Indian population. His total, for the territory extending from the upper Eel River to San Francisco Bay was 21,200, a figure in excess of the value conceded by ethnographers.

According to George Gibbs (1860, p. 118), the M'Kee expedition, on August 30, 1852, reached the Batimdakia (spelled also Ba-tim-da-kia) Valley, which was supposed to be at the head of the South Fork of the Eel River. John M'Kee implies that this valley was on the Middle Fork of the river but there is little doubt, judging from the route taken, that it was actually Long Valley, on the east branch of the South Fork. He says that the valley was inhabited by the Cabodilapo tribe and that a careful count showed 497 Indians. Since not all the natives could be located, John M'Kee estimated the actual population as 500 to 600. In a letter from Redick M'Kee to the commissioner in Washington, dated September 12, 1852 (1853, p. 185) it is stated that the population "may be" 600. M'Kee's counts, particularly in the Clear Lake Region, are generally regarded as too low. Hence his figure of 600 for Long Valley must be considered conservative. It should also be borne in mind that M'Kee saw only the east branch of the South Fork of the Eel River, which takes its origin in Long Valley. He did not get over to the west branch, which runs through Kato territory past Branscomb. Now Barrett shows eleven villages on the east branch and its tributaries, or an average of 55 persons per village. At the same rate the six villages on the west branch would add 330 for a total of 930 in the southern range of the Kato.

Heintzelman lists a group of seven names, representing Indian communities, which he says are up to 35 miles north of the site selected for the reservation, *i.e.*, Fort Bragg, or the mouth of the Noyo River. Heintzelman's distances and locations, as well as his names, are exceedingly hazy. Some of the seven names mentioned may refer to the northern Pomo, and some very likely pertain to the coast Yuki. Nevertheless two are undoubtedly Kato: the *Car-toos* and the *Ba-tims* (the former is cognate with Kato, and the latter must refer to Batimdakia Valley). The aggregate population is 700, according to Heintzelman. This is only slightly larger than M'Kee's 600. Allowing for conservatism on the part of M'Kee and over-liberality by Heintzelman, a fair estimate is 650. Alternatively, since Heintzelman saw the country three years after M'Kee had passed through, and the population may have diminished somewhat, the figure 700 secured by Heintzelman may well refer to both branches of the South Fork of the Eel.

For the Laytonville-Branscomb area we now have three estimates: by derivation from purely ethnographic data, 800; from the M'Kee reports, 930; and from the Heintzelman report, 700. Regardless of minor detail, the first method seems to yield results entirely consistent with direct contemporary evaluation.

Adding 300 to account for the remaining Kato territory we may retain the estimate of 1,100 for the tribe as a whole.

Kato ... 1,100

THE NONGATL, LASSIK, AND SINKYONE

For the three remaining northern Athapascan tribes we possess very little data of a strictly ethnographic character. Neither Kroeber nor Nomland (1935, 1938), who has studied some of these groups, have been able to secure any pertinent information regarding villages. Nor has Merriam been more successful. His list covering the region, under the title "Athapaskan Tribes, Bands and Villages Speaking the Nungkahl Language," mentions not more than two dozen villages in all and these are very widely scattered.

The entire failure of competent investigators such as those mentioned to come upon material traces of inhabited sites among these three tribes might be taken as indicative of a very small population. However, the existence of heavily inhabited areas to all sides of the region held by these tribes makes it unlikely that there was any large stretch of country which was devoid of a sizable Indian population. It is much more probable that numerous villages of the Lassik, Nongatl, and Sinkyone once did exist but that they were wiped out almost completely by the white frontiersmen in the early 'fifties before any observer left a record of them. As an indication of their fate may be mentioned the tales told by Bledsoe (1885) in his "Indian Wars of the Northwest" and by various witnesses in the Report to the California Legislature (1860) on the "Mendocino War."

When we are presented with such an entire lack of direct data, we are quite justified in falling back on the indirect area-density method. Thus the densities are tabulated below for the five other Athapascan tribes (including the Wailaki, considered subsequently) and for the Coast Yuki, a tribe in the region for which we have very accurate counts.

Tribe	Approximate area in sq. mi.	Population	Density in persons per sq. mi.
Chilula	210	800	3.86
Mattole	210	1,200	5.72
Whilkut	250	1,320	5.28
Kato	270	1,100	4.07
Wailaki	575	3,347	5.82
Coast Yuki	150	756	5.04
Mean			4.96

The close correspondence in density of the six tribes listed is noteworthy, and tends to lend confidence in the reliability of the ethnographic source material upon which these estimates are based.

The areas with which we are dealing are reasonably large; they are also relatively homogeneous in the ecological sense. All lie within the redwood-transition belt (except the Wailaki, which border it on the east), and all are characterized by small, perennial, salmon-bearing streams, along which the Indian villages were placed. There is nothing outstandingly different about the terrain occupied by the Lassik, Nongatl, and Sinkyone, except that perhaps it lies somewhat higher on the streams (but the Wailaki are still higher) and contains fewer flats and open valleys. The three tribes being considered had respectively 325 square miles, 700 square miles, and 615 square miles of territory. If the density was 4.96 persons per square mile the population would have been, to correspond, 1,612; 3,472; and 3,050. If we allow for a somewhat poorer habitat, these values may be reduced a little, say to 1,500; 3,300; and 2,900. It is difficult to see how the estimates can be carried much lower.

Nongatl, Lassik, and Sinkyone ... 7,700

THE WAILAKI

The Wailaki were studied by Goddard (1923, 1924), who published two papers concerning them. The first covered the main portion of the tribe along the Eel River and the second the Pitch group which lived along some of the tributaries of that river. Goddard found the Wailaki proper, as they may be termed, to consist of 18 communities or subtribes, each living in one to several villages, and the Pitch group to consist of 4 subtribes. One peculiarity of the villages was that they were inhabited only during the six winter months, the people in the summer dispersing through the hills in search of small game and plant food. Although the villages were occupied only half the year, nevertheless they can be used for computation of population since there were no other fixed abodes with which they can be confused.

In addition to Goddard's monographs, we have a tribe list for a portion of the Wailaki from Merriam entitled "Tsennahkennes Bands and Rancherias." Both investigators surveyed independently 11 of the 18 subtribal areas and obtained the names of villages from informants. In his list and in his text Goddard identifies 53 inhabited places. For two other subtribes, the Chiskokaiya and the Kaikichekaiya, he cites the villages by name in the textual descriptions There are a total of 18 for the two subtribes. Villages were not determined at all for the five northern subtribes.

For the first 11 subtribes Merriam gives a total of 46 villages. Of these, 30 can be identified with names furnished by Goddard, whereas 16 are in addition to Goddard's list. Goddard on the other hand gives 23 which were not secured by Merriam. Since both these workers operated carefully through informants and both were thoroughly conversant with the local dialects, we may accept the combined total of 69 villages, large and small, occurring within the territory of Goddard's first, or southernmost, 11 subtribes. The average is 6.27 villages per subtribe. For the Chiskokaiya and the Kaikichekaiya, Merriam mentions only one village each, that bearing the subtribal name. It is quite clear from his list that he did not push his field investigations into these groups. Hence we must fall back on Goddard's data, which include 18 villages in all. The average for the 13 subtribes therefore is 6.7 villages, and the total 87.

All the villages have long since been totally deserted and Goddard could count only house pits. (Merriam made no counts of any kind.) He did this for only two groups, the Baskaiya and the Slakaiya. Here he found and mentions twenty sites containing house pits. In all there were 92 pits but for two localities he specifies a certain number plus "several" others. If we allow 4 to represent "several" in each of these, then, the total number of pits is 100 and the average per site or village is 5.0.

Now since we are dealing here only with pits and not counts of houses remembered by informants, a reduction according to the Kroeber principle is justified for it is quite probable that all the houses once standing on the pits were not simultaneously occupied. When Kroeber has no other data, he recommends a reduction by one-sixth. I think that in this instance it would be proper to reduce by one-fifth, or 20 per cent. This would give an effective average of 4 houses per village. In the 13 communities covered by Goddard and by Merriam there were 87 villages, which at 4 houses per village would give a total of 348. No evidence is offered by either author to the effect that the remaining 5 subtribes differed in any essential way from the first 13. Hence we must ascribe to them 134 houses, making 482 in all.

We might use the Yurok family number 7.5, but Goddard's account carries the implication that perhaps the Wailaki family was somewhat smaller, suggesting a factor of 7.0 rather than 7.5. Goddard bases his estimates upon a mean population of 15 to 30 persons per village. This would mean 4.5 persons per house, certainly too low a value for the aboriginal social family. At four houses per village the family number would be 5.6, still probably somewhat too low. Perhaps a compromise is advisable, say at 6.0. The average village size could be then put at 25 persons, a figure definitely lower than was assumed for the more northerly Athapascan tribes but still one which seems to be indicated by the social organization described by Goddard. The total population of the Wailaki proper would then be 80 per cent of 482 houses multiplied by 6.0 or 2,315 persons.

Goddard indicates his belief that the villages were not simultaneously inhabited. However, he adduces no evidence to favor this view. On the contrary, he mentions in his text four villages which were stated by informants *not* to have been inhabited within their memory, a circumstance which argues strongly that the villages they did claim were actually active at the time to which they were referring, i.e., just before the white invasion. It would appear to the writer that reducing the house count by 20 per cent and reducing the family number from 7.5 to 6.0 quite adequately compensates for any errors in the ennumeration of villages. Indeed the estimate here presented may be too conservative.

With regard to the Pitch group Goddard (1924) shows that the subtribe tokya-kiyahan had 15 villages. In fourteen of these he found 66 house pits, an average of 4.72 per village. At tciancot-kiyahan there were 16 villages, 7 of which had 35 house pits, or an average of 5.0. Todannan-kiyahan had 6 villages but the area was incompletely examined and there were probably more. The area of tcocat-kiyahan was not seen at all but there is certainly no reason why they should not have had at least 6 villages. At four houses per village the total, surely an underestimate, would be 172 and at 6.0 persons per house the population would be 1,032.

For the entire Wailaki the indicated population is then 3,347 (or rather 3,350), a figure much in excess of previous estimates but justified by the data presented by Goddard and Merriam.

Wailaki ... 3,350

ATHAPASCAN TOTAL ... 15,450

THE YUKI

THE COAST YUKI

The Coast Yuki have been the subject of an admirable ethnographic study by Gifford (1939), who has assembled substantially all the data extant in modern times pertaining to families and villages. He shows very clearly that this tribe occupied its villages only in a transitory manner, that it had summer beach camps and inland winter settlements. To quote Gifford's words concerning the point

> I use the terms camp, hamlet, and village interchangeably in this paper. No site seems to have been occupied the year around. All were more or less temporary. The presence of an assembly house marked the more frequently occupied sites.

Hence it is necessary to examine Gifford's compilation of sites with as much care as possible in order to determine how many villages can properly be ascribed to the tribe.

It is also made clear in Gifford's paper that each of the eleven Coast Yuki groups had its own headman and ceremonial house. Each group had a frontage of seacoast together with a strip of territory which extended inland to the eastern limit of the tribe. Within this territory the group moved about with considerable freedom.

The following is a digest of the inhabited sites for the eleven groups. The groups are numbered (but the names omitted) in the order in which they appear of Gifford's paper.

> 1. One village is mentioned but no camp sites. For the group, therefore, the maximum number of sites occupied at any given time must be *one*.

> 2. Two "hamlets" are given by name. Since these are quite close together and in the same terrain, it may be assumed that *two* sites were simultaneously occupied.

> 3. Here are mentioned three camp sites and two villages (Esim and Melhomikem), one with 7-9 houses and the other with 8 houses. There was also a village which had been settled

after the coming of the white man, with 6 houses. It appears clear that aboriginally there were *two* semipermanent sites and a number of temporary settlements.

4. For this group Gifford mentions one beach village by name, one inland village, name unknown, and three camp sites. Although the beach and inland villages may not have been simultaneously occupied, the existence of three additional camp sites implies more people than would be contained in a single settlement at one time. Hence it is reasonable to regard the group as consisting of at least *two* village units.

5. There was one inland village with 6 houses (Onbit), one beach village (Lilpinkem) and one camp site with 8 houses. In view of the single camp site we have to regard the group as having *one* site occupied at a given time.

6. Here was one winter village and one beach village with no camp sites mentioned. Thus we may count *one* occupied site.

7. For this group there are known two villages, two hamlets, and one camp site, all with names. One hamlet had 3-4 houses and one village had 5 houses. Since there is no information on the location of the villages we may count all *four*.

8. *Three* hamlets are mentioned by name.

9. *Two* villages are mentioned by name.

10. *One* village mentioned.

11. *One* village mentioned.

The irreducible minimum number of villages therefore totals 20. It is quite probable that some of the other sites might be or ought to be counted but, since the evidence concerning them is equivocal, they will not be included. The house counts for seven sites average 6.3 and since we are here dealing with informants' memories of inhabited houses, not house pits, this number need not be reduced. With respect to family number, the Yurok value of 7.5 is probably too high. For the type of culture characteristic of the Coast Yuki the more conservative value of 6.0 is probably better. This yields a population of 756, or approximately 750. It is difficult to see how this estimate could be reduced.

Coast Yuki ... 750

THE YUKI PROPER

Although the Yuki were a populous and important tribe, and although Kroeber, in the Handbook, devoted three chapters to their culture, they have been the subject of but one special study. Quite recently G. M. Foster (1944) resurveyed their ethnography and worked out their village organization in some detail. He utilized informants who were in their seventies during the period of 1935 to 1940 and who thus were born no earlier than 1860. Since the social and political organization of the Yuki was completely disrupted during the 'fifties, particularly at Round Valley, it is remarkable that Foster was able to secure so much apparently quite accurate detail. It is true that certain specific items of information derived by Kroeber from his informants of thirty or thirty-five years earlier are more reliable than the comparable data of Foster, nevertheless the over-all coverage by the latter is more complete. Foster's account will therefore serve here as the basis for a computation of population.

There were eight major subdivisions or subtribes, the spelling of whose names and the precise boundaries of whose territories are slightly differently presented by Kroeber and Foster. Merely for convenience the description of Foster is followed here. Of the eight subtribes the most numerous and most important were the Ukomnom, who inhabited most of Round Valley. Next in importance were the Witukomnom directly to the south. Most of Foster's work was devoted to these two groups.

With respect to village organization Kroeber brought out the basic fact that the tribe was organized by communities, rather than separate and wholly independent villages (1925, pp. 161-162).

> The community always might and usually did embrace several settlements.... If designated it was referred to by the name of the principal village. This place name therefore designates at one time a cluster of several little towns and on other occasions one of these towns.

Foster went one step further and clarified the internal organization of the community. He showed that within each cluster there was always a principal village of relatively large size called the *nohot* with a constellation of small hamlets or, as he usually puts it, "rancherias" immediately adjacent. The former he likens to a host and the latter to a group of parasites. The nohot might contain as many as twenty-five houses and as many as 150 inhabitants. There might be anywhere from "2 to 6 to 8" rancherias per nohot. It is therefore possible, for certain subtribes, to obtain some idea concerning population from the list of inhabited places remembered by Foster's informants, particularly since Foster usually specifies what type of village is meant. This list is quite complete for the Witukomnom and the Ukomnom and partially so for the Tanom. Kroeber (1925, pp. 163-164) gives parallel data for a part of the Ukomnom, which can be to some extent brought into concordance with Foster's list.

The question of local population is difficult because in only one instance does Foster mention a specific figure: the largest nohot, which he says contained 25 houses and 150 people. It is of interest that elsewhere he states that the typical Yuki house would hold 4 to 8 persons. Thus he appears to accept without reservation a family number of 6. Now of course the average nohot was smaller and must have been intermediate between the maximum possible with twenty-five houses and the smaller villages which must have contained four or five. The halfway point is fifteen, a number which may be accepted with a fair degree of confidence. The nohot population would then be taken as ninety. The parasitic village or rancheria was definitely smaller. It could not have approached 15 houses yet by far the greater number of rancheria's must have had more than one or two. A reasonable compromise would be 4 houses and 25 inhabitants. With respect to the number of these hamlets per community the indefinite "2 to 6 to 8" may be set at four. Hence the community may be regarded as having on the average 190 inhabitants during pre-invasion times. There is no clear evidence to justify a larger estimate and on the other hand the whole context of both Kroeber's and Foster's discussion gives the impression of a group approaching 200 persons in number. This is somewhat but not materially greater than the mean number for the 22 subtribes of the Wailaki according to Goddard's data. That value was 153 and the subtribe among the Wailaki appears to have been very similar to the community among the Yuki.

For the Witukomnom Foster lists 15 places, of which 9 are designated as nohots and 6 as "small." Two points are apparent. First, the informants of Foster were recalling the *important* villages which they had seen or been told about but had forgotten the minor sites, hence the great preponderance of nohots. In the second place, it is unnecessary for purposes of calculation to know the names or the number of the peripheral "parasitic" rancherias if we know the primary towns, the nohots, for, knowing a nohot, we know a community. Thus we may immediately set the population of the Witukomnom as at least 1,710 persons. If the informants gave incomplete data, then the number would be higher.

For the Ukomnom Foster lists 38 place names, most but not all of which lay in Round Valley. Of these 6 are specified as nohots. This would yield as a first approximation a population of 1,140. But for the Ukomnom we have some help from Kroeber. Many of Foster's remaining places are designated merely "rancheria," since his informants could remember no further details. For one of them, Kroeber says that there was a dance house present, which makes the site a nohot instead of a rancheria. Kroeber's group B includes the village of Pomo, which is not mentioned by Foster. This was the seat of a head chief, and therefore a nohot. In addition, Kroeber includes in this group 6 villages in Willliams Valley. Foster says regarding "Flint Valley," by which he is evidently referring to the same locality, that his informants could remember no villages. This seems to be an instance where Kroeber's earlier informants could recall villages which Foster's later ones had forgotten, for there is no ground for doubting the accuracy of Kroeber's work. There is no implication that any of these sites was large, hence they may be regarded as the small type of village with about 25 persons apiece. We can therefore count 8 nohots plus 6 rancherias, which gives a population of 1,670 for the entire group.

A further check on the Ukomnom is provided by Foster's map of Round Valley. In the valley proper he shows 37 inhabited villages, of which 25 are named and 12 are unnamed. Of the former, 7 are known to have been nohots. Taking the nohots at 90 persons and the other sites at 25 persons, one gets a total population of 1,380. A balance of 300 is by no means excessive for Williams Valley and the peripheral hills. Incidentally, this figure for Round Valley yields a density of roughly 45 persons per square mile, one which surpasses any other in California but one which is quite in accord with all the accounts of early settlers and explorers.

The Tanom, living on the Eel River to the northwest, are credited by Kroeber with six "divisions," the names for which he gives. Foster lists also six names, which he says are "probably districts named after the principal rancheria" There is no doubt that both authors are referring to communities or, as Kroeber calls them, "political units." Hence at 190 persons their aggregate population would have been 1,140.

For the other five subtribes we have very little direct information. Among the Huitinom Foster knows of two nohots and two rancherias, all at considerable distances from each other. The country was rugged but the area large and served by Black Butte Creek, a fishing stream with several tributaries. Two nohots and two rancherias would indicate a minimum of 330 people. It would not be excessive to place the number at 400.

The Suksaltatamnom lived to the northeast on the headwaters of the South Fork Eel River, close to the Pitch Wailaki. They are all dead and nothing whatever is known of their villages. Their number may be tentatively placed at 400, since in all other respects their habitat resembled that of the Huitinom.

On Onkolukomnom lived to the southeast in a large area centering around Lake Pillsbury. There are none left but Foster thinks "they are undoubtedly numerous." Certainly they must have exceeded the two preceding subtribes and an estimate of 600 should not be too much.

The Lalkutnom and the Ontitnom lived close together south and west of Round Valley. Regarding the former Foster says there were "a number of nohots and rancherias." If we allow four to be "a number" and assume that the rancherias were all subordinate to the nohots, the population would have been 760, a not excessive estimate. The Ontitnom, as far as Foster could determine, consisted of one nohot or, let us say, 200 persons.

Yuki proper ... 6,880

THE HUCHNOM

This important subdivision of the Yukian stock lived along the South Eel River and its affluents from a point below the junction with Outlet Creek to the head of Potter Valley, at which region they merged with the Pomo. They were a river people, with their villages all placed on the banks of the Eel and one or two of the larger tributaries.

The original modern ethnographic account of the Huchnom was by Barrett (1908), whose description of villages is accepted almost verbatim by Kroeber in the Handbook. A more recent account, derived from one informant, is given by Foster (1944, pp. 225 ff., App. 1).

Barrett describes and shows on his map 13 villages, of which 11 are on the Eel and 2 on Tomki Creek. Of the former 5 are located close together along the boundary between the Huchnom and the Northern Pomo. This territory is shown on Foster's map as being within the confines of the Pomo; hence some confusion might arise, were it not that both Barrett and Kroeber are very positive in ascribing the sites to the Huchnom, not the Pomo. Barrett's map is undoubtedly more accurate for this area than Foster's.

Barrett calls all these "old village sites," as opposed, for example, to modern inhabited villages. He makes no distinction as to size. Kroeber in taking over Barrett's list refers to them as "main settlements." Foster states that "village organization and society in general were about like the Yuki." Hence it could be inferred that the 13 places were all of the nohot type, and thus that a total population of 2,470 is implied.

This may not, however, be entirely justified. Kroeber says *settlements* not *communities* and Barrett says *villages*. Reference therefore may have been to individual dwelling places not to groups or constellations. Foster begs the question entirely by referring merely to the work of the previous investigators as "ample." On the other hand, if the Huchnom organization was similar to that of the Yuki, as Foster avers, then at least some of the names mentioned must have been community capitals, or nohots, the smaller villages peripheral to which have been forgotten.

We have a few additional items which are helpful. The northernmost village, *cipomul*, is said by Foster's informant to have been the residence of a "captain." Hence it was a principal village or nohot. Three villages are stated by Barrett (and so shown on his map) as having been located on both banks of the Eel River. Such extension suggests a size greater than that of a small parasitic hamlet, whether or not they may be regarded as nohots. Moreover the distribution of Barrett's sites along the river is interesting. According to his map, the line of 11 villages along the stream, disregarding minor meanderings of the latter, extended about 40 miles. From the northern border and going upstream there are 6 villages in the first 25 miles, the minimum distance between any two being 3 miles. Since the usual distance between a primary village and its satellites among the Yuki, according to Foster, is not more than a mile or two, none of these 6 settlements can have been of the secondary type. The cluster of 4 named towns along the 5 miles of river at the extreme south were quite close together, and not more than 2 of them may have been of this type. At the headwaters to the extreme east there was one definitely isolated village, which may be placed in the larger category, as may also the two sites on Tomki Creek. Of the 13 places given by Barrett there is therefore reason to believe that at least 11 were of the nohot variety.

Indirect confirmation of this conclusion comes from comparison of the Huchnom village distribution with that of the subtribes of the Yuki proper. The Tanom had 6 nohots scattered along approximately 20 miles of the Eel River and the Witukomnom had 4 or 5 along some 15 miles of stream valley. The Huchnom territory was about 270 square miles and, judging roughly from the maps of Foster and Barrett, the Tanom and the Witukomnom areas were approximately 200 square miles each. The Tanom possessed at least 6 nohots and the Witukomnom 9 (Foster's data). Hence the average area covered per nohot would be 33 for the Tanom and 22 for the Witukomnom. If we allow 11 primary villages or nohots for the Huchnom the average area covered by each would be 25, entirely within the same range. Now the character of the terrain for the three groups did not differ in any essential respect. Hence there is no reason to suppose that the population density of the Huchnom, computed on a riparian or area basis, was any less than that of the other two subtribes. Furthermore I can see no evidence pointing to a smaller individual community or village population among the Huchnom. Eleven nohots or village constellations would yield a total population of

2,090, or approximately 2,100, an estimate somewhat smaller than the one given previously but one which I can find no reason for further reducing.

Some confirmation of the figure derived from village data is contained in the survey of Heintzelman (1855). He mentions as one of his principal divisions the Bi-lo-ki, a name which is the same as Balokai. The latter were the Pomo of Potter Valley, according to Kroeber and also Barrett This group, Heintzelman says, included 3,000 persons. However, he breaks them down into six smaller divisions and says that "these Indians reside between Clear Lake and the heads of Eel, Russian and Trinity Rivers." The six divisions are: Tar-toos, Si-dam, Po-ma Pomes, Si-mas, Di-no-kis, and Du-che-calla-os. The Si-dam and Po-ma Pomes are undoubtedly Potter valley Pomo. The Si-mas, according to a personal communication received from Dr. Barrett, are probably Yuki from the region of the headwaters of the South Eel River (the tcimaia mentioned in the Ethnogeography of the Pomo, 1908. p. 247). The Di-no-kis and the Du-che-calla-os Dr. Barrett is unable to identify. The Tar-toos are undoubtedly Huchnom (see Barrett's monograph, 1908. p. 256; also confirmed by personal communication). Their number is given by Heintzelman as 1,600. This value, for 1855, bespeaks an aboriginal population not far from 2,000. Hence again the ethnographic method is supported by the estimate of the contemporary observer.

Huchnom ... 2,100

YUKI TOTAL ... 9,730

THE ATHAPASCANS AND THE YUKI

If we total all the Yukian divisions, including the Coast Yuki and the Huchnom, we get 9,730 persons. Similarly, the Athapascan tribes collectively give 15,450. The combined total is 25,180. Some of the groups, such as the Tanom and Huchnom, may have been overestimated, but this will be compensated by underestimates for other groups, such as the Onkolukomnom. If we accept as valid the published ethnographic data of Barrett, Kroeber, Foster, and Gifford, together with the manuscript material of Merriam, it is very difficult to fix the population of the Athapascan and Yukian stocks at a figure much below 25,000.

In this connection it is interesting to consider the estimates of Heintzelman, because his figures for the Kato and for the Huchnom have been shown to conform in general to those derived from village lists.

Many of Heintzelman's Indian names cannot now be identified and his localities are frequently vague and obscure. However, a reasonably clear line can be drawn between the Pomo and those tribes living north of the Pomo.

The first five groups mentioned in the report are unequivocally Pomo. Then come the "Bi-lo-ki, Po-mes" with the six divisions previously mentioned called Tar-toos, Si-dam, Po-ma Pomes, Si-mas, Di-no-kis, and Du-che-calla-os. The Si-dam and Po-ma Pomes are Potter Valley Pomo. The Tar-toos are Huchnom. The Si-mas are probably southeastern Yuki. The Di-no-kis and Du-che-calla-os cannot be identified by Dr. Barrett (personal communication) and are therefore probably not Pomo. Since the whole group was said by Heintzelman to reside "between Clear Lake and the heads of Eel, Russian and Trinity Rivers" these two unidentified divisions may be ascribed to the Yuki. The numerical aggregate of the four Yukian divisions is 2,450.

Following the Bi-lo-ki on Heintzelman's list are the Me-che-pomas who inhabit the east part of Kinamoo Valley and the "Eel River Mountains," 40 miles northeast of the proposed site, i.e., Fort Bragg. Covelo is almost exactly 40 airline miles northeast of Fort Bragg. Barrett (1908, p. 249, fn.) says that the Pomo name for Round Valley is maca-kai, and quotes another variant, Me-sha-kai. In a personal communication he states his belief that Round Valley is here referred to. Along with the Me-che-pomas Heintzelman lists the Be-dar-ke-sill, which he says are found in the south part of Trinity County and the north part of Mendocino County, 50 miles from Fort Bragg. Since the name cannot be identified, the people may be allocated on the basis of location alone to the southern part of the Wailaki. The aggregate population of these two groups is given as 2,100.

The next seven names on Heintzelman's list are the Car-toos, Ba-tims, Kab-in-a-toos, Kon-ispilla, Koss-ill-man-u-pomas, Kam-ill-el-pomas, and So-as. These are all stated to be north of the selected site, Fort Bragg, with the most remote tribe 35 miles away. In his textual statement Heintzelman says that he went up the coast as far as Cape Mendocino, but from his times and distances it appears more likely that he reached approximately the Mendocino-Humboldt County line before turning eastward and going inland. This would bring him just about 30 or 40 miles above Fort Bragg.

It has already been pointed out that the first two names of this group. Car-toos and Ba-tims, refer to the Kato. Dr. Barrett thinks that the third name, Kab-in-a-toos, may possibly be the Kabenapo of Clear Lake. He says (personal communication):

> We know that the Lake people visited the coast. Perhaps
> Heintzelman encountered some of these kabenapo over on
> a salt-gathering expedition to some point on the coast north
> of Fort Bragg.

If Barrett is correct, then this tribe must be excluded from the present enumeration. The Kon-is-illa cannot be traced, yet the name has definite similarity to the Coast Yuki name (Pomo form) Kabesillah, as given by Kroeber in the Handbook Koss-ill-man-u-pomas cannot be identified, but Barrett says that Kam-ill-el-pomas is the same as kamalal pomo, a name given by the Pomo to the Coast Yuki (1908, p. 260). The term So-as is thought by Barrett to refer to the village sosatca in Sherwood Valley.

All these groups are clearly stated by Heintzelman to lie north of Fort Bragg. Nevertheless, in view of the possibility that Kab-in-a-toos may represent Clear Lake inhabitants and that the So-as may be a village in Sherwood Valley, and hence be Pomo, these two divisions may be omitted from consideration. The remainder may with considerable safety be ascribed either to the Coast Yuki, the Kato, or perhaps the Sinkyone on the coast above the Yuki. The total for the five divisions is 1,700 persons.

The next five names on Heintzelman's list are quite definitely Northern Pomo. Then come, as the last two tribes, the Ki-pomas and the Yo-sol-pomas. The former were said to inhabit Kinomo Valley, 40 miles from Fort Bragg, and the latter to live on the coast 50 miles north of Fort Bragg.

According to Barrett, the Ki-pomas are probably the Kai Pomo of Powers (1908, p. 279, fn.). If so, they lived not in Kinomo Valley (Round Valley) but in the area between the headwaters of the South Fork of the Eel River and the Middle Fork of the Eel. Thus they must have been Athapascan, whether Kato, Sinkyone or Wailaki, it is now impossible to say. The Yo-sol-pomas are probably the Yu-sal Pomo of Powers, who were an Athapascan people near Usal, on the coast above Westport (see Barrett, 1908, p. 260).

The Ki-pomas and the Yo-sol-pomas had a combined population of 2,200. Thereafter Heintzelman says: "From the Yo-sol-pomas to Eel River on the north, and east to the ridge from Humboldt to Kin-a-moo Valley there cannot be less than four thousand...." The area thus delineated is very ambiguous. It may be taken roughly, however, as embracing—according to the general map in Kroeber's Handbook—the southern third of the territory of the Mattole and Sinkyone, together with that of the Kato and the Wailaki. To this must be added the region which includes all branches of the Yuki.

The population estimates based upon the village lists of the ethnographers are as follows: one-third the Sinkyone, 970; one-third the Mattole, 400; the Kato, 1,100, the Wailaki, 3,350; and the Yuki as a whole, 9,730. The general total is 15,550. By comparison Heintzelman's figure for approximately the same area is 12,450. Considering the imponderable and unassessable factors involved in both computations the correspondence is remarkably close, particularly in view of the fact that Heintzelman was not in the region until 1855, at which time the population was by no means aboriginal.

THE POMO

From a poverty of ethnographic material with the more northerly tribes we pass to an embarrassment of riches with the Pomo. (Barrett, 1908; Gifford, 1923, 1926; Gifford and Kroeber, 1937; Kniffen, 1939; Stewart, 1943). The first major study was that of Barrett in 1908. Barrett's principal contribution was a painstakingly compiled list of Pomo tribes, villages, and camp sites as recalled by his informants during the years 1903 to 1906. However he missed the significance of the Pomo community style of social organization with its implications for evaluation of village size and importance and hence probable population. Moreover, many of his place names have since been shown to be wrongly applied. His work remains therefore chiefly valuable as a compilation and check list against more recent and more critical work.

Gifford's two papers (1923, 1926) stand as models of investigation of a single social unit, the village of Cigom. They are useful in a wider sense as a point of departure and a basis for comparison with other communities, particularly in the Clear Lake region. The work of Gifford and Kroeber (1937), although primarily dealing with cultural matters, contains much pertinent information concerning the sixteen communities investigated together with several paragraphs pertinent to the population problem.

Kniffen (1939) made a careful study of the geographical and ecological status of certain selected groups: the Clear Lake area, the Kacha of Russian River, and the Coast Pomo. Steward (1943) reviewed the boundaries and villages of all groups except a few on Clear Lake, using also the ecological approach.

When one attempts to establish what were the Pomo community groups and chief villages, he encounters a great deal of divergence of opinion on detail among these investigators, due largely to differences among informants. Without extensive field work, which might in fact now be impossible, many of the discrepancies cannot be resolved. On the whole, the later students appear to have come closer to the truth and are probably more reliable.

CLEAR LAKE POMO

Gifford said (1937, p. 122) that there were 11 communities on Clear Lake. Kniffen reorganized them to make 12, after which Stewart returned to a count of 11. This last number, therefore, may be accepted as final. Each of them consisted of a single principal village of considerable size. A classical example is Cigom. Other inhabited spots within the community area have usually been recognized but whether they were permanent or shifting villages or camp sites usually is not clear. For this reason the population has been discussed by ethnographers since Barrett simply on the basis of the group, without much reference to the number of sites known to have existed. The single exception I would make to this procedure is to take account of the number (not necessarily the names and location) of the villages known to have possessed assembly houses, since the presence of these implies some degree of permanence. A community with one capital village and several such accessory sites would, other things being equal, create the presumption of a larger aggregate population than a community with a capital village and one or no subsidiaries.

There is a more definite population estimate for the Clear Lake region than we have for many other native groups. L. L. Palmer in his History of Napa and Lake Counties (1881), cites figures for the aboriginal population of the Clear Lake communities which he obtained from an informant who could well remember the days before the advent of the white man. These figures have been subject to some disparaging criticism by more modern students. The chief objection advanced is that the book is one of the many county histories which appeared as commercial ventures in the 1880's and which, on the whole, were very carelessly written. Palmer, however, as his text shows, was much interested in the fate of the natives and took considerable pains to secure informants who could give him data. There is no ground for impugning either his honesty or his competence. Moreover, it is difficult to see why informants seventy years ago should be any less reliable than they are now. Hence I can see no reason for not accepting his figures as they stand, subject to the limitations of his informant's knowledge.

With regard to those limitations it should be noted that the informant was a native of the Kulanapo community on the west side of the lake. He should therefore have had closest acquaintance with his own people and the adjacent group, the Habenapo. His figure for the Kulanapo was 500, a value which Kniffen attacks on the ground that Palmer's informant intentionally exaggerated the importance of his own group. This is a wholly gratuitous assumption and inconsistent with the fact that, since more was known at that time about the west-shore people, his figures could easily have been checked, had they been widely at variance with the facts. In the second place, the figure for the Habenapo was given as 300. Now Barrett (1908, p. 194) quotes even more specifically from Palmer:

> The Hoo-la-na-po (Kulanapo) tribe was just below the present site of Lakeport.... At one time there were two hundred and twenty warriors, and five hundred all told in the rancheria. They are now reduced to sixty. Sal-vo-di-no was their chief before the present one, Augustine.

If we are going to discredit the testimony of the chief concerning his own village thirty years previously, we had better throw out along with it the information secured from septuagenarians who have to recount at second hand what their forefathers told them.

Some confirmation of Palmer's figure for the Habenapo is given by Barrett (1908, p. 195), who mentions a statement from the Report of the Commissioner for Indian Affairs in 1858 referring to the Lupillomi. The latter in turn are identified by Barrett as the Habenapo. The Commissioner said: "Upon the Lupillomi ranch, near Clear Lake, there are some three hundred Indians." Although by 1858 there may have been some reduction and mixing of population, the identity is striking.

Although the figures of Palmer's informant may be relied upon for his home territory at the southwestern corner of the Lake, for the north, east, and southeast shores he may have been inaccurate, being less familiar with those sections. The chief evidence for such a conclusion lies in the discrepancy between his figure for Cigom and that secured by Gifford after a meticulous and exhaustive examination of every individual who had lived in the village. Palmer's figure is 160 whereas Gifford's is 235. Thus Palmer's informant clearly underestimated, by a ratio of 2 to 3. Hence it is not unreasonable to increase Palmer's figures for the communities remote from the area of his informant.

If we ignore for the moment Palmer's data and neglect individual differences between communities, it would be possible to take Gifford's figure of 235 for Cigom as representing the average for a Clear Lake community. The population of the area would then be 2,585. Let us, however examine the eleven communities individually (following Stewart's outline, 1943, App. 1, pp. 57-59).

1. *Bachelor Valley and Tule Lake.* Stewart gives Cinal as the principal village with Homtcati and Xaro as villages with assembly houses. In his text he says that these villages plus Mamamamau "were occupied under the leadership of one chief." Hence there were at least three secondary or subsidiary "occupied" villages. In addition, in footnote 30 to page 41 he points out that Kniffen had set apart a portion of the area under the name of Yobotui. Kniffen (1939, p. 368) gives the Yobotui the status of an independent group and shows a principal village under that name on his

map. The group, whether single (Stewart) or compound (Kniffen), was clearly of quite large size. This is in line with Palmer, whose informant gave a population of 120 for most of the group but set apart Yobotui with an additional 150. Stewart's group, with two possible main and two or three subsidiary villages, is credited by Palmer with 270 people. Since the area lay in the extreme north, this estimate may be raised, in conformity with the Cigom case, by 50 per cent, making 405.

2. *Scott's Valley.* There were two groups here just prior to white settlement. The first was designated as the Boalke, Boilkai, or Yimaba, with one principal village Karaka (Stewart) or two "significant winter villages," Noboral and Karaka (Kniffen). Palmer's informant said they had 180 people and, since they lived near him, his figure may be accepted without change. The other group were the Komli, which are placed as a separate group by Stewart. All authorities agree, however, that they were Russian River natives who in relatively recent times migrated to Scott's Valley. Palmer says they had 90 people, a reasonable figure. The total for the two groups is thus 270.

3. *Upper Lake.* Here was a well defined group, with only one village, Xowalek. The History of Lake County gives them 150, which because of the distance from Lakeport may be increased to 225.

4. Another group in the same vicinity was the Danoxa, with a principal village of the same name plus either two or three villages with assembly houses. Palmer says they had 100 inhabitants, which may be increased to 150. From the number of villages it might be supposed that Danoxa was larger than Xowalek. But in giving the figures Palmer's informant may have confused the two groups; 375 seems a reasonable value for the two together.

5. *Clear Lake, east.* Gifford's value of 235 may be accepted without further comment for Cigom.

6. *Lakeport.* The status of the Kulanapo has already been discussed. Palmer's figure of 500 seems reasonable.

7. *Kelseyville.* The Habenapo are assigned a population of 300.

8, 9, and 10. *Lower Lake.* The three groups inhabiting the entire region of the southeast were the Kamdot, Elem, and Koi. Each had a principal village plus from two to four others with assembly houses. They are in the same terrain with and appear to be quite similar to Cigom. Palmer gives for the three a total population of 390, which, if increased by 50 per cent, would mean 585. If, on the other hand, we regard them as being of the same character as Cigom we could multiply 235 by 3 and get 705.

A curious contributory bit of evidence can be derived from Gifford's study of land ownership in this area (1923). Gifford shows that the ownership of property at Cigom was communal but at Kamdot, Elem, and Koi, it was a family matter. He lists very carefully the exact ownership of the tribal real estate. There were 22 tracts belonging to the *village* of Cigom but 85 belonging to *families* of Elem, 38 to *families* of Koi, and 57 to *families* of Kamdot. From this we can derive the minimum number of families for these places, for the tracts were simultaneously owned by different families. Using a factor of 6 persons per family the population of Elem would be 510. In this connection it is of interest that Gifford during the same investigation found that two subsidiary villages were occupied simultaneously with the main village. Thus he states "A second mainland overflow village, which was once *contemporaneously inhabited* with insular Elem and mainland Behepkobel, was Mucokol...." (Emphasis mine.) A principal village the size of Cigom or larger plus two accessory villages of only 100 each would bring the population to 435. Thus there can be little doubt that Elem had fully 500 inhabitants. On the basis of family number the figures for Koi and Kamdot would be respectively 228 and 342, or, say, 230 and 340.

According to the data above the total population of the Clear Lake basin was 3,155, which may be rounded off to 3,150. When Kroeber originally formulated an estimate of the population of the Pomo communities, based largely upon Barrett's study, he set the average per community at 100. Later (Gifford and Kroeber, 1937, p. 119) he reduced the probable number of communities and reset the population limits at 75-300. with a likely average of 200. The average we get here is 287, considerably larger than Kroeber would allow. However, all the available evidence seems to support the conclusion that, for the Clear Lake region at least, the community size was somewhat larger than stated by Kroeber.

A puzzling secondary question is what disposition to make of the Lileek, the small Wappo group associated with the Habenapo. These people came very late and settled among the Habenapo, probably after the effect of the white invasion farther south had begun to be felt. Palmer's informant said there were about 100 of them. They might be added to the Habenapo but, in view of the doubt concerning their origin and history, it is perhaps best to disregard them entirely.

Clear Lake Pomo ... 3,150

NORTHERN POMO

For the remainder of the Pomo we have no such clearly defined body of knowledge as for the Clear Lake group. Thus it is necessary to consider each subdivision or subtribe separately. As a preliminary step, however, it is desirable to discuss the problem of house and family number in so far as it relates to the Pomo.

In Gifford's analysis of Cigom we possess a remarkably thorough treatment of the demography of a single village, one which may be taken as representative of the entire tribe, with the exception of the portion lying along the coast. At Cigom Gifford found 47 social groups or families and 235 persons. The mean is 5.0 persons per family. However this figure represents the period of 1850 and immediately thereafter, when the Clear Lake population had already for several years suffered from contact with the whites. Hence the aboriginal value must have been higher. Indeed Gifford's study gives an amazing picture of the demographic dissolution of the Pomo in the mid-nineteenth century.

Among the 47 families there were 57 persons who were described as "son" or "daughter" and were obviously at or below the age of puberty at the period the informants were recalling. This means only 1.21 children per family, far below the minimum number (2.0) necessary for replacement. Clearly the population was declining rapidly at that time. If there were 1.21 children and the family number was 5.0, the average number of adults was 3.79. For simple equilibrium or stability, such as we must assume existed in pre-white times, at least 3 children must be found in every family. Thus with 3.79 adults there would have to have been a family number of 6.79 or say, 6.80 merely to maintain the population. Considering the relative richness of the environment and the quite elaborate culture of the Pomo an average of 7.0 is by no means excessive for the aboriginal Pomo.

That the Clear Lake Pomo were in a deplorable state at the time described by Gifford is attested by the statements of his informants concerning the subsequent fate of the 57 children mentioned in the text. Of these, 29, or 50.9 per cent, "died young." Such a tremendous child mortality is quite consistent with our entire picture of the postcontact decline in Indian population but is wholly at variance with any reasonable concept of aboriginal conditions.

At Cigom Gifford found 20 houses, mostly of the multiple type so common among the Pomo. Three of the houses held 4 families, three held 3, twelve held 2, and two held 1. The average is 2.35 families per house or, in terms of persons, 11.75 per house. This is of course based on the 1850 value of 5.0 persons per family. If we admit an aboriginal number of 7.0 persons per family, then the number per house becomes 16.45 instead of 11.75.

In his study of Redwood Valley Kniffen (1939, pp. 373-380) puts the population at 125 and the number of houses at 12. This would mean 10.4 persons per house, quite close to Gifford's value for Cigom in or near 1850.

In his chapter on the Pomo Stephen Powers (1877) described the village of Senel (Sanel, Shanel) in the Russian River valley (p. 168 and map). He shows on his map 104 houses and 5 assembly houses. The houses were large and contained according to his estimate 20-30 persons each. This estimate seems much too high. However, on other grounds he puts the former population at 1,500 inhabitants, a figure which is arrived at entirely independently by an informant of Stewart (1943, p. 45). Indeed Stewart comments with reference to Powers that "my population estimate and description closely approximate his." This means for 104 houses a mean of 14.42 occupants.

The average of the three sets of data available give 13.76 persons per house, a figure which may be rounded off at 14.0 in view of the probability that Kniffen's estimate is a little low. It is noteworthy, furthermore, that neither Gifford nor Powers gives any indication that all the houses in the villages respectively studied were not simultaneously occupied. Indeed, with the multifamily system it is difficult to see how they could stand deserted for a considerable period of time.

The Potter Valley groups.—Stewart paid particular attention to the Potter Valley groups and determined the central or capital villages to have been Canel, Sedam, and Pomo. Stewart also says that, whereas Canel was the main village in its area, Yamo was the most populous. Sedam was one of the largest villages in the valley and Pomo was somewhat smaller. By comparison with the Clear Lake towns it is appropriate to consider the three principal towns (including Yamo with Canel) as having approximately 200 inhabitants each, or 600 in all. The next question concerns peripheral or outlying villages, of which there were certainly a considerable number. Stewart says that the Canel were "distributed" among 12 villages (including Yamo). Moreover "my informant (JSm) insisted that these villages were all occupied at the same time ... each having a 'curing' sweathouse; however all were under one chief, and there was only one ceremonial or 'devil' house" Barrett (1908, fn. 129, p. 142) says his informant called three of these villages camps only. At the same time Barrett lists 9 villages, excluding Kachabida and Canekai, 6 of which correspond to villages of Stewart. Merriam lists 10 villages, only one of which is in addition to those of Barrett or Stewart. Although there is some overlap, it seems clear that there were at least 12 villages apart from Canel, Sedam, and Pomo. Of these Yamo has already been considered. Kachabida, mentioned by Barrett and Merriam, was one of those which migrated to the Clear Lake region shortly before 1850 and must therefore be excluded, since its people have already been counted among the Clear Lake Pomo.

Canekai lay several miles to the northeast in the hills. It is simply shown by Stewart on his map as lying in the territory of Sedam. Merriam, however, calls it a "small tribe," the shanel-kaah, and cites Gibbs (1860), who mentioned the group under the name of the Shanelkaya. Evidently a fair-sized village or minor subtribe once existed in the area. At least 100 persons must be ascribed to it

Deducting Yamo, Kachabida, and Canekai and three of Stewart's villages which Barrett said were camp sites there remain 11 villages supported by the word of at least one of the three above-mentioned authorities. Five are given by all three of them, 4 by two of them and 2 by one alone. It is safe therefore to allow 10 villages in addition to the 5 already accepted (i.e., Canel, Sedam, Pomo, Yamo, and Canekai). Concerning the size we have no data but they must all have been relatively small. Three houses each would seem a reasonable estimate, yielding at the Pomo rate of 14 persons per house 42 inhabitants for each village or 420 for the aggregate. Thus, counting 600 for Canel, Sedam, Pomo, and Yamo, 100 for Canekai, and 420 for the balance, we get 1,120 as the best estimate for the Potter Valley subtribes.

Calpella and Redwood Valleys. — This area is divided by Stewart into two subtribes, the Masut of Calpella and the Katca of Redwood Valley. This course is also followed by Kniffen who made a special investigation of the Kacha (Katca). On the other hand Merriam included both groups in his tribe, the Mah-soo-tah-ka-ah (his manuscript entitled "Northern Pomo").

The Kacha tribe all lived in the village given as Kacha by Kniffen and as Kabelal by Barrett, Merriam, and Stewart. Kniffen says "there must have been about 125 people in the valley...", but gives no supporting data. He does, on the other hand, mention that the village had 12 houses (1939, p. 375). At the aboriginal Pomo number of 14.0 there should have been 168 instead of 125 inhabitants. It is quite possible that Kniffen was thinking in terms of the early 1850's and hence made a low estimate. It appears to the present writer that 170 is preferable.

Masut is given by Barrett and Stewart as a village but by Merriam as a tribe. Another village near by, Chom-cha-de-lah (Merriam) or Chomchadila (Powers, Kroeber) is admitted by Stewart and in fact given as the main village in his appendix. Stewart also adds two villages, Diskabel and Kobida. It is evident that there were several villages closely clustered together. Stewart thinks there were four. Of these Masut and Chom-chah-de-lah were apparently large and the others perhaps small. We may allow 150 each for the larger ones and 50 each for the smaller, making 400 in all.

The village of Matuku lay in the same territory. This is given the status of tribe by Merriam but was involved in the migrational movements between the Calpella region and Clear Lake. Hence its population is difficult to evaluate. Perhaps 100 persons will be adequate.

In near-by Coyote Valley lived the tribe called by Powers the Shodokaipomo. This seems to be the general name for the subtribe and perhaps also for one of their villages (Barrett and Merriam). In addition, Merriam, following Barrett, lists Shah-chahm-kah-oo (called Shashamkau by Kroeber). Powers (1877) in commenting on this group has this to say: "Mr. Christy states that there were between three hundred and four hundred (people) when he arrived." Since there is no specific reason to doubt Mr. Christy's word, we may set the population of the subtribe at 350. The total for the entire area is 1,020.

There are for the Calpella-Redwood Valley region 8 reasonably well authenticated villages, as follows:

> Kabelal (Barrett, Merriam, Stewart)
>
> Masut (Barrett, Stewart)
>
> Chom-cha-de-lah (Powers, Barrett, Merriam, Stewart, Kroeber)
>
> Matuku (Barrett, Merriam, Stewart)
>
> Shodo-kai (Barrett, Merriam, Powers)
>
> Shah-chahm-kah-oo (Barrett, Merriam, Kroeber)
>
> Diskabel (Stewart)
>
> Kobida (Stewart)

Of these five may be regarded as principal villages and hence large; the others may have been small. The average for all together is 127 persons per village. If we allow 175 persons for each of the larger ones, we must assume 50 for the smaller. These figures seem of the correct order of magnitude.

Willits Valley.—The tribe inhabiting Willits Valley extended from the inland valleys clear to the coast. Stewart makes it clear, however, in contradistinction to Barrett, that they had no permanent villages actually on the coast before they moved in that direction ahead of the American advance to the north. The Northern Pomo thus, unlike the Coast Yuki, lived a long distance inland and traveled to the seashore only as occasion demanded from time to time.

Stewart lists 9 village sites: Mitom, the principal village; Tsamonda, a small village; Nabo; Talel, with 8 dwelling pits; Tsaka, with 8 pits; Bakau; Cotsiu; Kacebal; and one of unknown name. He says that there is no evidence that all these were occupied at the same time, but "several must have been occupied simultaneously because five were occupied by the parents of Indians still living."

Much light is thrown on the situation in Willits Valley and adjacent areas by the work of Merriam (in the manuscript "Northern Pomo"). Merriam splits the natives into three dialectic subgroups: the But-kow-hah-po-mah of upper Outlet Creek, the Sho-jul-po-ma of eastern Little Lake Valley, and the Met-tum-mah of Willits Valley proper.

The But-kow-hah-po-mah had a principal village But-kow-hah-chut-te, corresponding to Stewart's Bakau plus "3-4 rancherias." If we allow 150 for the main village and a possible 25 each for the outlying rancherias, we get 250 for the group. This seems quite reasonable for a small, somewhat isolated subtribe.

The Sho-mul-po-mah had for a principal village Sho-tse-yu-chut-te, which is mentioned by Barrett and corresponds to Stewart's Cotsiu. In addition, Merriam cites from Barrett 6 other villages, 4 of which he confirms as villages. One of these, Tah-nah-kum-chut-te, he says contained a sweathouse having a capacity of 200 people. According to a principle enunciated by Powers, but which is of somewhat doubtful validity, the capacity of a sweathouse or assembly house is equivalent to one-third of the population. Thus the Sho-mul-po-mah might have had 600 people. However, if we allow that the principal village, by analogy with Kasha, had 175 and that each of the villages of Barrett which were confirmed by Merriam had 4 dwelling houses each (i.e., 56 people) then the population would be computed at 400.

In the Mitom region Merriam is very explicit. He mentions Me-to-mah-chut-te, which corresponds to Stewart's Mitom, and says that it was the "name applied by Me-tum-mah to all their villages in Metumki of Little Lake Valley. There were 4 important permanent winter villages containing about 600 people." These 4 villages were, according to Merriam: Cha-bo-cha-kah-chut-te, Po-ka-hil-chut-te, She-o-kah-lau-chut-te, and Tsah-kah-chut-te. The last corresponds to Stewart's Tsaka. Of the first village he says it contained 40 to 50 house pits. This must be excessive for it would mean a population of 560 persons in this village alone. Stewart says that Tsaka had 8 pits, or 112 persons. If we reduce the count for Cha-bo-cha-kah-chut-te to 300 instead of 560, we can still accept Merriam's figure of 600 for the group of four.

We still have to account for Kah-be-shal-chut-te of Barrett and Merriam (Stewart's Kabecal), Tsam-mom-dah-chut-te of Barrett and Merriam (Stewart's Tsamonda). Nabo of Merriam and Stewart (also mentioned by Gibbs). and Talel of Stewart. Talel and Nabo may have been part of the Mitom complex but Tsamonda and Kabecal are too distant. If Tsamonda was small, as Stewart says, we may allow 50 inhabitants. Kabecal must have contained at least 100.

For the entire area, including all three of Merriam's linguistic groups, we get a population of 1,650 inhabitants.

Sherwood Valley. — In this valley lived the Mato or Mato-poma of Stewart, or the Mah-to-poma of Merriam, whose permanent villages were inland but who ranged a large territory extending to the coast. According to Stewart there were three minor divisions of the group, with three permanent villages, Mato, Kabedile, and Kulakau, each of which had its own chief. On no other evidence would we be justified in ascribing 200 persons to each subgroup. Stewart says "The best guesses of my informants placed the primitive population at about 500 persons, half of them in the main village of Mato." That would give 250 to Mato and 125 each to Kabedile and Kulakau. This estimate appears too low, particularly since the informants were all born in the 1860's, twenty years after the first contact with the white man.

Merriam (in his "Northern Pomo," together with a separate manuscript entitled "Sherwood Valley rancherias") transcribed and checked Barrett's village list. As was his custom he initialed in ink those names which he confirmed by independent investigation, leaving unmarked those for the existence of which he considered he had no certain evidence. For Sherwood Valley he gives 25 names. Of these, 3 were taken from Barrett without confirmation, leaving 22. Seven of the latter are given by Merriam alone, in addition to those appearing on Barrett's list. Merriam mentions Mah-to-chutte and also Ma-chah-tah, each of which he says was a "big rancheria." It is very probable that these were variants of the same name or were parts of the same village. Hence they may be combined as representing Stewart's Mato. Merriam also mentions Kah-ba-de-la-chut-te and Kah-baht-be-dah-chut-te, which appear to be variants for Stewart's Kabedile. Also included are Bo-shahm-koo-che (Bocamkutci), Cha-bo-tse-y-chut-te (Kabotsiu), and Tan-nah-shil-chut-te (Tanacil), all of which are stated by Stewart to have been parts of Kulakau. This reduces Merriam's effective list to 17.

Mato is stated by Merriam to have been a "big rancheria." This is in line with Stewart's impression that the village contained at least 250 persons. This number may therefore be accepted without much hesitation. Kabedile (or Kah-baht-be-da-chut-te) is said by Merriam to have had 30 to 40 house holes. He also mentions the fact that the Mexicans perpetrated a massacre here in 1846, in the course of which 25 were killed and many children stolen for slaves. If we take the lower limit mentioned for houses and reduce one-third, we still get a probable 20 houses, which at 14 persons per house gives a minimum population of 280 persons. Stewart gives Kulakau and the three villages considered to be parts of it equal rank with Mato and Kabedile. Merriam says of Cha-bo-tse-y-chut-te (Kobotsiu) that it was a "big village." Hence we may safely ascribe 250 persons to the town.

Merriam adds certain comments on the villages. Doo-lah-kah-chut te had a "big round house." Che-ah-po-y-chut-te was of "fair size but no roundhouse." She-ko-ki-chut-te consisted of "two big rancherias and roundhouse." The other 10 villages are listed merely by locality without additional information. We encounter here a clear instance of the perplexity which pursues us throughout the Pomo area. We must accept either the combined word or Barrett and Merriam that there were numerous subsidiary villages inhabited in Sherwood Valley during aboriginal times or the word of Stewart that there were not. At this point it must be emphasized again that by 1840 the Northern Pomo had been invaded by Spanish-Mexicans from the San Francisco Bay region and their aboriginal social order had been partially disrupted. Furthermore, we know that they had been exposed to serious inroads by disease, such as the great smallpox epidemic of the 1830's. In particular, that of 1837, the so-called "Miramontes epidemic," began at Fort Ross and is known to have seriously involved the Russian River Valley. There is much reason to believe, therefore that the population decline began by 1830, with its accompanying shifting and consolidation of villages. Both Barrett and Merriam did their field work among the Pomo from 1900 to 1910, say as an approximate date 1905. A seventy-year-old informant at that time could thus actually remember the year 1840. But a similar individual in 1935 could remember of his own knowledge only to 1870. He would have to draw on second- and third-hand information imparted by his forefathers. As Stewart says of one of his Sherwood Valley informants his "father's father told JMc of 'old times'." It is hardly to be expected that an old man could very accurately transmit population data secured as a small boy at his grandfather's knee. For these reasons I think Merriam's village names cannot be discarded, unless specific evidence proves that they are errors. They must be accepted as villages which at one time were inhabited. There remains of course the possible contingency that some of these places had been abandoned before the advent of the first white influence or that they were spots inhabited for a short time during the upheaval accompanying the American invasion. Since there is no conceivable way in which we may ascertain the true facts in detail, perhaps some arbitrary correction is desirable. Consequently the following procedure is suggested: estimate the population on the basis of all the Merriam names, then reduce by one-third. Such a method should take care of all instances of temporary villages, camp sites etc.

Applying the above principles, we may assign 150 inhabitants to Boo-tah-kah-chut-te ("big roundhouse"), 50 to Che-ah-po-y-chut-te ("fair-sized but no roundhouse"), and 200 to She-ko-ki-chut-te ("two big rancherias and roundhouse"). Two houses, or say 30 persons, may be allocated to the other 10 sites of Merriam. The total would then be 700, which, reduced by one-third, gives as a final value 470.

For the Mato-pomo as a whole the population figure is 1,250. It is difficult to see how a much lower figure could be set for the area.

For the Northern Pomo collectively there has been derived a population estimate of 5,040. It is of interest to compare this figure with the values cited by Heintzelman.

This officer listed eight names which can be indentified as falling within the group being discussed. They are as follows.

> 1. *Si-dam.* This is *sedam* of Barrett (1908, p. 141) and of Stewart (1943, p. 41), located in Potter Valley.

> 2. *Po-ma Pomes.* This is *pomo* of Barrett and Stewart, likewise in Potter Valley.

> 3. *Kal-il-na-pomas.* This group was located between Martoo (Sherwood) and Metumki (Little Lake) valleys and is possibly equivalent to kalal-nokca, a village below Ukiah (Barrett, personal communication). However the habitat specified by Heintzelman does not support Barrett's surmise. The group undoubtedly lived much to the north of Ukiah.

> 4. *She-bal-na-pomas.* These were in Sherwood Valley and are referred to by Barrett (1908, p. 147, fn.) as the Shi-bal-ni Pomo.

> 5. *Calli-tal-pomas.* Dr. Barrett is unable to identify the name but the people lived in the same vicinity as the tribes mentioned previously. It is possible that they may have been the *kabelal* of Stewart (1943. p. 39).

> 6. *Yo-pomas.* Dr. Barrett thinks (personal communication) that this term may signify *Yo kai pomo* ("south valley people") who would have lived near Ukiah. But Heintzelman states that they lived between Kinomo (Round) Valley and Martoo (Sherwood) Valley, and hence must have been Northern Pomo.

7. *Maa-to-ma-pomas.* With regard to these people Dr. Barrett writes me as follows: "Possibly refers to Little Lake or Willits Valley people *mtomkai*, or *bitomkai* (1908, p. 128, fn.), or to *milomu*, on a knoll in the town of Willits (ibid., p. 145)." The latter hypothesis appears the more probable (Stewart, 1943, p. 36 ff., discusses this subtribe at length). Heintzelman adds the information that the Maa-to-ma-pomas are divided into seven tribes, of which the *Sho-he-shas* are the most numerous. Barrett (1908, p. 146, fn.) thinks that the latter people are the Chow-e-chak of M'Kee. Heintzelman further says that the territory covered extends from Metumki (Little Lake) Valley to the coast.

8. *So-as.* Barrett considers (personal communication) that this name refers to the village of *sosa-tca*, in Sherwood Valley (cf. 1908, p. 147).

Irrespective of conflicts in terminology it appears that Heintzelman fairly well covered the area usually assigned to the Northern Pomo under the eight designations just listed. His total population value is 5,350, slightly greater than but very close to the estimate derived from ethnographic data (i.e., 5,040). This close correspondence will be seen as specially significant when we come to examine his report on the Central and Southern Pomo.

Northern Pomo ... 5,040

CENTRAL POMO

Ukiah. — In the Ukiah area are included four of Stewart's subtribes: the Yokaia of Ukiah Valley, the Ciego of Largo, the Cokoa of Hopland, and the Yobakeya of Echo. There are all consolidated by Merriam in his manuscript entitled "Tribe List of Yo-ki-ah Pomo" and will be considered together.

Stewart is very positive that these four tribes all lived in one central village. He says regarding the Yokaia: "Although several villages are given by Barrett for this area, there is no doubt that during the winter months the population was concentrated in one main village". Regarding the Cokoa: "Politically, as well as geographically, the Cokoa resembled the Yokaia. Both had a single central village of importance where the population was concentrated" Merriam credits Barrett with 37 village names, to which he adds none himself. Of the 37 he confirms only 13. Since the other 24 of Barrett are doubtful, they may be excluded. Of Merriam's 13 Stewart says specifically that three were camps not permanent villages. Two, Kah-chi-o (Katcayo) and Shah-na-na-oo (Caneneu) were proved by Stewart to have existed only subsequent to the white invasion. One may belong to the Booneville tribe and another is a tribal, not a village, name. Four, Kah-ka-eu (Cokadjal). Ko-lo-ko (Koloko), Lema (Ciego), and Shanel (Canel) were the main villages, as stated by Stewart. There remain unaccounted for only Bok-shah (Barrett's Bokca), regarding which Merriam says it had a sweathouse and was "practically permanent," and Katch-a-wah-low. Merriam's conclusions thus coincide to a remarkable degree with those of Stewart and justify the assumption that, where the two investigators clearly differ, considerable weight should be given to Merriam's account.

The largest of the four main villages was Canel, or Shanel. Comment has already been made upon the fact that both Stephen Powers' and Stewart's informants, proceding from entirely different premises, reached the conclusion that the town had a primitive population of 1,500. This figure therefore, however incredible, must be accepted. It is noteworthy in passing that if we apply the family number of 14 to the 104 houses shown by Powers on his map of the town, the population is computed at 1,456, almost identical with the other estimates.

For the Yokaia, originally settled at Cokadjal, Stewart says: "The population ... has been variously estimated at from 500-1,000 persons...." Since such estimates are likely to be somewhat low, and in view of the size of Canel, we may take the upper limit, 1,000 inhabitants.

The status of Lema (Ciego) is dubious. Stewart says the people had no chief and the tribe was composed of "soldiers." The town was very well known at the time of white occupation, however, and must have held at least 150 persons.

The Yobakeya at Koloko were also warlike and Stewart calls them a "small group." But he also says that one of his informants told him there were about 60 survivors of the tribe in his youth (approximately 1865). This fact argues an aboriginal membership of at least 300 persons.

For the Yo-ki-ah linguistic subdivision of the Northern Pomo as presented by Merriam the collective population is thus estimated at 2,950.

Point Arena.—The Point Arena area is a large territory comprising 300 square miles along the coast. Stewart designates its occupants the Bokaya and includes three subtribes centering in the villages of Kauca, Pdahau, and Lacupda. Merriam separates two groups, the Bo-yah, which included Kauca and Pdahau, and the Kan-no-ah, or the Lacupda people ("Tribe List of Bo-yah" and "Tribe List of Kan-no-ah").

One of Stewart's informants, a woman born about 1880, said that the aggregate population was 380. This appears much too low. Merriam lists 29 villages, of which many are taken from Barrett without confirmation.

On the other hand Stewart says regarding Pdahau: "there is no doubt that other villages were occupied contemporaneously with it, although it was impossible to get the exact status of all the sites mentioned by Barrett." Hence the acceptance of some of Barrett's and Merriam's villages must be considered.

Merriam's list includes Stewart's three main villages. It also includes Itcetce and Kodalau, which Stewart says were settled after the American occupation. Merriam also gives the following, some of which are on Barrett's list:

1. Kah-bim-mo ("permanent village")

2. Kah-sha-lem ("permanent village, large town. Inhabitants moved many years ago to Cha-cha. Used as slaves by man named Shoemaker.")

3. Kah-sil-shah-ko ("acorn camp and winter rancheria")

4. Kah-ya-a-lin ("acorn camp and winter rancheria")

5. Kup-pish-ko ("permanent village")

6. Shah-dah ("permanent village")

7. We-chahl (of the Kan-no-ah, "very large permanent village")

The remaining 17 village names are credited to Barrett without comment or confirmation.

Suppose we accept the values put on Pdahau, Kauca, and Lacupda by Stewart's informant, i.e., respectively 200, 100, and 80. Then we should allow 150 each for Merriam's "large" villages, nos. 2 and 7 above. The other five were apparently small and may be conceded 30 persons each. Of the final 17 sites it will be fair to admit the probably simultaneous existence of two-thirds of them, or let us say 12, at the rate of 30 persons per village. The total for the area then becomes 1,190 inhabitants. Using Stewart's figure of 300 square miles for the area the density would thus be 3.97 persons per square mile or less than Gifford found for the Coast Yuki. Such an estimate seems extremely conservative.

Booneville and Yorkville. — In this area are found the Pdateya of Booneville, which Stewart puts among the Northern Pomo, and the Danokeya of Yorkville. The corresponding names used by Merriam are the Lah-ta and the Ta-bo-ta. Very little is known of either group. Stewart mentions the village of Lemkolil near Booneville and Late and Maboton in the Yorkville region. Merriam gives Barrett's list (in his manuscript entitled "Ta-bo-ta and Lah-ta") without comment. For the Ta-bo-ta there are 10 villages and for the Lah-ta 9. Since we have absolutely no other leads we may assign the three main villages 100 inhabitants each, and deduct one-third from the remainder to allow for Barrett's nonpermanent sites. There would then be 10 presumptive villages with 30 persons each, or 300 for all of them. The total population for the two groups together would then be 600.

Stewart's Point.—The tribe at Stewart's Point is known as the Kacia (Stewart) or the Kah-chi-a (Merriam, manuscript entitled "Tribe List of Kah-chi-a pomo"). Also included are Stewart's Yotiya of the Southern Pomo, a group for which I find no account in Merriam's notes.

Stewart has made a particularly exhaustive study of this group and states that the population range extended from 800 to 1,200 persons. Merriam gives 82 names of villages. Stewart makes it quite clear that aboriginally the Kacia had no permanent settlements on the coast itself. All their villages were at least four or five miles inland, except Mitini and Powicana. We must delete therefore all the coastal villages of Barrett and Merriam except the two mentioned. This immediately removes 27 names, leaving 55. Of these, 16 are mentioned by Stewart as "villages which were occupied more or less permanently" Five of them had assembly houses. Of the remaining 39 sites, 30 are confirmed by Merriam from Barrett's list or are given by him in addition to Barrett. If we consider that the larger, known population of the villages such as Mitini balances errors in Merriam's list and the mean number of persons per village was 30, then the total for the group is 46 times 30, or 1,380. To this should be added, according to Stewart, 100 for the Yotiya, making 1,480 in all. This is somewhat, but not excessively, greater than Stewart's estimate.

For the Central Pomo as a whole we may turn once more to the record left by Heintzelman. For the area here being considered he lists five tribes.

> 1. *Uk-a-is.* These are stated to be located "above the canyon of the Russian River," and are obviously the villages grouped around Ukiah. A discussion of the Yokaia is given by Stewart (1943, pp. 43-45).

> 2. *Sinals.* This term clearly refers to the village of Shanel, already mentioned with respect to population.

> 3. *Bo-kas.* These were located "in the vicinity of Fort Ross" and included no doubt the Bokeya of Point Arena as well as the survivors around Fort Ross.

4. *Ta-bi-tas.* These were "in Anderson's Valley" and refer to the inhabitants of the village Tabate (Kroeber and Stewart) or to the group called the Pdateya by Stewart.

5. *Bo-i-os.* These were located "south of Booldam River on the coast," in other words south of Big River near the boundary between the Northern and Central Pomo.

Since the region of Ukiah, Hopland, Booneville, Point Arena, and Fort Ross was well explored and even extensively settled by 1855, it is entirely probable that Heintzelman recorded all the existing natives of the area. Regardless of terminology the five names above leave no important fraction of the territory unaccounted for. Heintzelman's total for the population is 2,100, a figure which should be compared with the value of 6,220 obtained through the use of village lists, together with house and family number.

For the Athapascan and Yukian peoples, as well as for the Northern Pomo, a marked correspondence could be observed between the two sets of data, even though entire identity could not be achieved. For the Central Pomo, on the other hand, there is a striking disparity: the Heintzelman estimate reaches only one-third the value obtained from ethnographic sources. Since Heintzelman could reach his maximum accuracy among the relatively well known Central Pomo, as opposed to the remoter northern groups, we cannot ascribe his low count to ignorance or carelessness on his part. The most reasonable explanation is that the Central Pomo had already by 1855 suffered a reduction in population of from one-half to two-thirds of the aboriginal level. Such an hypothesis is entirely consistent with all we know of Mexican and American settlement in Sonoma and southern Mendocino counties and, furthermore, tends to lend support to the much higher figures reported by Heintzelman for the more northerly tribes.

Central Pomo ... 6,220

SOUTHWESTERN POMO

This group, consisting principally of the Kacia of Stewart's Point, has already been discussed under the Central Pomo.

SOUTHERN POMO

In this area lived five large groups, named variously by different students, centering around Dry Creek, Cloverdale, Healdsburg, Santa Rosa, and Sebastopol. The Pomo residue, mentioned by Barrett, and others who survived in Alexander Valley are here omitted since they may be more appropriately considered as contributing to the predominantly Wappo population. Likewise, the village of Wilok, east of Santa Rosa, is probably considered more satisfactorily in conjunction with the neighboring Wappo.

Modern ethnographic data are of little value for estimating the population of the Southern Pomo, however carefully it may have been secured. The Spanish and Mexican missionaries, accompanied by the military, entered the area certainly before 1820 and by the year 1835 the Southern Pomo had been relocated in the missions, conscripted for labor, or carried off by disease. Shortly after 1840 the Americans began to appear and as a result the original village pattern was completely disrupted. Hence it is relatively useless to compute population from the sites which in recent years have been remembered by Indian or white informants. Merriam, following Barrett, lists about 80 village names but in very few instances endorses Barrett's findings by subscribing his initials. To attempt any detailed analysis of these sites would serve no useful purpose whatever.

It is clear from the opinions expressed by Kroeber and Stewart that the Southern Pomo exhibited the same general type of social organization as the Central Pomo, namely, a splitting into subtribes with each of the latter inhabiting a single, large main village. Several of these have been reasonably well identified, some by modern ethnographers and some by the early missionaries and civil contemporaries. There are 15, the existence of which is sufficiently well assured. They are as follows:

1.	Amalako	Dry Creek	Stewart
2.	Amako	Cloverdale	Stewart, Merriam
3.	Makahmo	Cloverdale	Stewart, Merriam, Kroeber
4.	Amatio	Healdsburg	Stewart, Merriam
5.	Kale	Healdsburg	Stewart, Merriam
6.	Mukakotcalg	Healdsburg	Stewart, Merriam
7.	Wotokkaton	Healdsburg	Merriam, Kroeber
8.	Tsoliikawai	Healdsburg	Stewart, Merriam
9.	Batiklechawi	Sebastopol	Merriam, Kroeber
10.	Masikawani	Sebastopol	Stewart, Merriam
11.	Hukabetawi	Santa Rosa	Merriam, Kroeber
12.	Kabetsiuwa	Santa Rosa	Stewart, Merriam
13.	Gualomi	Santa Rosa	Mission records, Merriam

14.	Chichiyomi	Santa Rosa	Mission records,
				Merriam
15.	Levantoyome	Santa Rosa	Mission records,
				Merriam

If each of these fifteen villages had a population of only 300 Indians, a low value considering the huge congregations in the Ukiah-Hopland region, the total for the Southern Pomo could be set at 4,500.

There is a little contributory evidence to be obtained from the mission records. These documents, which are to be found in the Bancroft Library of the University of California, include baptism records for the missions of San Rafael and Solano, those which drew upon the Pomo for converts. Up to 1834 there had been baptized 268 persons from Levantoyome, 90 from Gualomi, and 44 from Chichiyome. Conversions in peripheral areas like that of the Southern Pomo were always far from complete, particularly at the end of the mission period. Many of the natives were killed in the incessant skirmishes and massacres of the time, many were enslaved directly by rancheros, many died of disease, but by far the greatest number simply fled the approach of the white man. It is quite reasonable to suppose that not more than one-third of the natives were ever actually brought into the missions for conversion. This would mean an average of 402 persons for the three subtribes or villages just mentioned, Levantoyome, Gualomi, and Chichiyome. Extended to the entire 15 known principal villages, the total would be 6,030.

A second possible method consists of area-density comparisons. The over-all density in the sum of the Potter Valley, Calpella, and Ukiah areas can certainly have been no greater than that originally existing in the region of the Southern Pomo, for of all the Pomo subdivisions the southern group possessed the most favorable habitats and the most prolific food supply. The population found for the three northern areas mentioned above was 5,090 and the area according to Stewart was 585 square miles. The density was thus 8.70 persons per square mile. The corresponding value for the Clear Lake Pomo is 7.34. The area of the Southern Pomo, including the five groups discussed here was 745 square miles. At the northern density of approximately 8 persons per square mile the population would have been 5,960.

The two methods employed therefore yield essentially similar results and make possible the estimate of 6,000 persons for the Southern Pomo.

According to Alexander Taylor (1860-63, Ser. I, folio page 5) Captain J. B. R. Cooper, an American, went to Santa Rosa as early as 1827. Apparently following his statements Taylor says "it was estimated" that 2,000 Indians lived in Sonoma Valley and 1,500 in Santa Rosa Valley. In another place (Ser. I, folio page 3) Taylor states that "when Capt. Cooper settled the Molino Rancho, in Santa Rosa Valley, in 1834, there were living in his neighborhood as many as 2,000 Canimares." The latter term refers of course to the southeastern portion of the Southern Pomo.

We should not accept these pioneer estimates of Indian population without examination and qualification. Neither should we reject them, equally uncritically, as automatically exaggerated and mendacious, and hence worthless. It is quite likely that Cooper knew more about the number of Indians on his ranch than any other white man, at the time or since. It is relatively unlikely that Cooper had any motive for propagating a completely false report. On the other hand, it is wholly possible that Cooper may have been inaccurate or careless in his count. Nevertheless the Cooper estimate is quite in conformity with our other sources of population information.

It was stated previously that 402 baptisms are on record from three rancherias in the Santa Rosa area. To these may be added 220 others whose names are clearly Pomo in character, making a total of 622. At the rate of three aboriginal inhabitants to one baptism in this region, the territory concerned — and this is very close to Cooper's home — would have contained 1,866 people. The mission data thus in general support Cooper's figure.

Cooper says that in 1834 there were "in his neighborhood" 2,000 Canimares. Since the Molino ranch embraced the region north of Sebastopol and west of Santa Rosa, his "neighborhood" may be considered as including the Sebastopol and Santa Rosa groups of the Southern Pomo, leaving the Healdsburg, Cloverdale, and Dry Creek groups beyond his horizon. The estimates cited by Taylor refer rather ambiguously to the period between 1827 and 1834, let us say roughly 1830. The earliest Pomo conversions which are recognizable from the mission records were at San Rafael in 1820. These Pomo had therefore been subjected to intense missionization for at least ten years prior to Cooper's appearance. The population consequently must have been seriously depleted when he first saw the Santa Rosa Valley.

If we disregard entirely the factor of depletion and accept Cooper's 1834 estimate of 2,000 Canimares around Santa Rosa and Sebastopol, we may allow an equivalent population for the other three Southern Pomo provinces. This yields a total of 5,000. If we attempt to make any correction for depletion, we very quickly reach the figure already arrived at by other methods, viz., 6,000.

That a comprehensive population reduction was in progress throughout the era of 1820 to 1850 and later is attested by the report of Major Heintzelman.

His figure for the Northern Pomo, it will be recollected, was definitely within the range of the population determined from ethnographic data. His value for the Central Pomo was only one-third of that computed by other methods, and the discrepancy was accounted for on the basis of the decline in numbers from the first white contact to 1855, the year of Heintzelman's trip. At the end of his report he makes the statement that "south of the Cañon of the Russian River there are about eight hundred indians." In other words, the Southern Pomo (which all lie south of the canyon) had dwindled to no more than 800. The converse may also be maintained. Since Heintzelman had a very good check on the population of the well-settled south and since, according to all known testimony, the attrition among the Indians of this area had been appalling during the preceding 30 to 40 years, it follows that the original population must have been very much greater than that conceded by Heintzelman. Hence a level of several thousand may be accepted.

Southern Pomo ... 6,000

NORTHEASTERN POMO

This little tribe, living on the border of the Sacramento Valley, has never been investigated thoroughly. Barrett (1908) listed 13 rancherias but Merriam's informants (manuscript entitled "Sho-te-ah or Northeastern Pomo Tribe and Villages") allowed only 7. At 50 persons per village this would indicate a population of about 350.

Northeastern Pomo ... 350

SUMMARY

The figures advanced here give the Pomo as a whole a population of 20,760 individuals. This is three times Kroeber's estimate but conforms to the general level found in this review of the Northwest California tribes.

POMO TOTAL ... 20,760

THE COAST MIWOK

According to the maps shown by Barrett (1908) and by Kroeber (1925), the Coast Miwok occupied an area of approximately 885 square miles in Marin and southern Sonoma counties. A projection of the Pomo value of 8.0 persons per square mile would give 7,080 for the Coast Miwok, a result which appears much too high.

A careful collection of former village sites through modern informants has never been possible, even at the beginning of the present century, because Marin County was infiltrated by the Spanish and the Indian life was thus disrupted at a very early date. Indeed the first recognizable Coast Miwok baptism was at San Francisco in 1783. Barrett and Kroeber have assembled, to be sure mainly from the tradition handed down to informants by their ancestors, a quite impressive list of villages. Barrett (1908, pp. 303-314) gives 36, and Kroeber on his map (1925, p. 274) shows 42. If we arbitrarily assigned a population of 100 each, we would have a total of approximately 4,000, probably somewhat too high a value. The difficulty is that we have no clear means of gauging the size of the typical Coast Miwok village, since no informants have been able to give a precise figure and since the terrain occupied by this tribe is different from that held by the Pomo to the north.

Even though the investigation of villages yields no very fruitful results, the Mission records for the Coast Miwok provide a quite adequate solution of the problem.

Unlike any other tribe north of San Francisco Bay the Coast Miwok were thoroughly and completely brought into the missions. Beginning, as indicated above in 1783, gentiles from the north shore were brought in small numbers to the Mission Dolores for conversion. In 1817 San Rafael was established, and within a few years the missionaries had made a clean sweep to the coasts of the bay and the ocean and had begun to penetrate north to the vicinity of Santa Rosa and Sebastopol. Meanwhile a considerable number of converts had been taken to San Jose, and subsequently some found their way to Sonoma. Fortunately we have the baptism records, or their equivalent, of all these missions.

Identification of the Coast Miwok can be made in most of the records (1) by the year and the location (e.g., the year 1817 at San Rafael); (2) by village names identical with or similar to those listed by Barrett and by Kroeber; (3)

by linguistic affinities (such as the prefix *echa-* or the suffix *-tamal*); and (4) by subsidiary notes in the records indicating geographical location. Deleting all really doubtful cases we have the following numbers of baptisms

San Francisco	896
San Rafael	916
Solano	48
San Jose	162

The total is 2,020 persons.

A baptism at any of the four missions constituted a net withdrawal of one person from the native community, since all converts from the immediate vicinity of the missions could be easily kept at the mission establishment or could be recaptured without difficulty if they escaped. Hence the total baptism number must very closely approximate the total population of the area over a period of forty years. But the wild population was undoubtedly decreasing owing to other causes from, say, 1790 to 1830. The presence of the Spanish soldiers or missionaries always introduced diseases and caused disruption of native society to such an extent that the death rate outran the birth rate. Hence the new converts were being drawn from a diminishing population.

Another factor is fugitivism. Intimate contact with the white man for a long period taught the native what to expect in the missions and on the ranches. Consequently there always was a fraction of the Indian community which eluded the best efforts of the missionaries and which made good its escape beyond the periphery of Spanish and Mexican influence. Many of these natives never returned to their original homes. Still other sources of attrition were the kidnaping of adults for labor on the ranches during the 1820's and the promiscuous killing of all sexes and ages during the frequent armed encounters between white men and red men.

Although for the Coast Miwok the above-mentioned causes of loss cannot be assessed numerically with any approach to accuracy, nevertheless their total effect must have been considerable. As a purely arbitrary but essentially reasonable guess we may say that they produced a one-third reduction in the net aboriginal population. Then, if the remaining two-thirds was baptized, the initial value would have exceeded 3,000. This is twice the figure selected by Kroeber (1925, p. 275) who says that "the Coast branch may have numbered 1,500." Yet it is difficult to see how, with a total baptism count of over 2,000, the aboriginal level could have been any lower than 3,000.

COAST MIWOK ... 3,000

THE WAPPO AND THE LAKE MIWOK

These two ethnic groups are combined, together with the small corner of the Wintun living in the lower Napa Valley, in order to complete this survey of the area north of San Francisco Bay.

Direct area comparisons between the territory here concerned and that held by the Pomo and the Coast Miwok can lead to only very tentative conclusions. If we use the region delineated by Barrett (1908) on his large-scale map, the peoples mentioned above occupied approximately 950 square miles of land surface. The density of population was reckoned for the Pomo at 8.0 per square mile and that for the Coast Miwok, with a population estimated at 3,000, comes to 3.4. The equivalent estimates for the Wappo and Lake Miwok would be respectively 7,600 and 3,260. There are no grounds for immediate decision whether either is too high or too low. Consideration of the character of the terrain is not very helpful since the Wappo-Lake Miwok habitat resembled that of the Pomo in some respects and that of the Coast Miwok in others. We must therefore turn to other devices.

In contrast to the Coast Miwok the Lake Miwok and the Wappo have been the subjects of ethnographic studies of direct value to the population problem, particularly those of Barrett (1908) and of Driver (1936). In considering these data, and also those furnished by the mission records, it will be desirable to split the region into six small areas along the lines indicated by the map given by Kroeber in the Handbook (1925, pl. 27, opp. p. 172). Hence we have (1) the Lake Miwok, (2) the Western Wappo, (3) the Northern Wappo, (4) the Central Wappo, (5) the Southern Wappo, and (6) the Wintun of Napa Valley. As a starting point we may select the Western Wappo.

The names and the location of the villages differ widely as presented by the three investigators of the area. The confusion is rendered even more profound because Barrett in his terminology takes account of the Pomo occupancy of Alexander Valley in the early years of the nineteenth century, whereas Merriam and Driver ignore, not only the presence of the Pomo, but also the names applied by them to settlements. On the other hand, Driver's study is the most thorough of them all and for this reason alone may well serve as the basis for consideration of population. Driver lists (1936, pp. 183-

184) 10 places which he calls "permanent towns." Of these, one is located outside Alexander Valley and hence may be disregarded; two are cited as of "unknown" location and thus had better be disregarded also. There remain seven, all of which Driver places on his map They are set forth below, together with the names given by Merriam and Barrett which cannot be reconciled with those of Driver.

> *Kotico-mota* (Driver). Koticomota is mentioned by Barrett (1908. p. 271) as having been taken from the Pomo by the Wappo and occupied by them. Probably the largest town in Alexander Valley.

> *Nets-tul* (Driver). This village is not mentioned by Barrett under this name, although it is located near Barrett's Cimela and Koloko. Its existence, however is confirmed by Merriam who calls it Net-tool.

> *Owotel-peti* (Driver). This was located near the two preceding villages on the east bank of the Russian River, in the vicinity of Barrett's Cimela and Koloko. Driver mentions two summer camp sites, the people of which lived here during the winter. Its status seems assured.

> *Pipo-holma* (Driver). This was the northernmost village in the valley. Barrett says this was an aboriginally Wappo town and took the lead in the war with the Pomo.

> *Tsimitu-tso-noma* (Driver). Driver says that this was a "small town" with no sweathouse, and that the people sweated at Unutsawaholma. The name was not known to either Barrett or Merriam and it is quite possible that it was a summer camp, or a temporary site, or merely a suburb of one of the other villages. Its existence as a permanent settlement is open to some doubt.

> *Unutsawa-holma-noma* (Driver). This town also is not listed under the given, or any similar, name by Barrett or by Merriam. However, in view of the exhaustive study made of it by Driver its existence is indisputable. It may be represented by the Cimela or Koloko of Barrett.

> *Osoyuk-eju* (Driver). This is the only village shown by Driver as lying west of the Russian River. Barrett gives no similar name but Driver reaffirms its active existence by the mention of a summer camp site the people of which lived in Osoyuk-eju in the winter.

Holko-mota (Driver). This is given by Driver as a camp site and probably is identical with Holko-a-cho, which is called a rancheria by Merriam. Driver's opinion is to be followed and the place should be regarded as a summer camp.

Hut-mitul (Driver). A camp site.

Nuya-hotsa (Driver). A camp site.

Tcano-nayuk (Driver). A camp site.

Ts'awo-tul (Driver). A camp site.

Tico-mota (Driver). A camp site.

Halio-wahuk-holma (Driver). A camp site.

Walma-pesite (Driver). A camp site.

Ko-tish-hal (Merriam). Listed by Merriam as a rancheria, but we have no further information concerning it.

Too-la-chil-le (Merriam). A rancheria, but no further information.

Cimela (Barrett). The Southern Pomo name is *ossokowi*. This village was formerly occupied by the Pomo but the Wappo took possession after the war. It undoubtedly corresponds to one of the villages placed by Driver at approximately the same spot on the east bank of the Russian River.

Koloko (Barrett). This village was said to have been located near Cimela. Regarding it the following quotation from Barrett is decisive "In addition to these villages along Russian River which were occupied by the Wappo, names of four other sites were obtained which, as far as can be learned, were not occupied by the Wappo but were occupied by the Southern Pomo before the Wappo took possession of this section, and for which only Pomo names could be obtained." It is clear therefore that the village as such had disappeared prior to the knowledge of Driver's informants, if indeed these villages had ever been occupied by the Wappo.

Malalatcali (Barrett). See Koloko.

Acaben (Barrett). See Koloko.

Gaiyetcin (Barrett). See Koloko.

From this list there emerge six villages as certain. Driver's Koticomota, Netstul, Owotelpeti, Pipoholma, Unutsawaholma, and Osoyukeju. Of these Osoyukeju, on the west bank of the river, may be regarded as having replaced Barrett's three villages, Malalatcali, Acahen, and Gaiyetcin, which evidently did not survive Pomo occupancy. Driver and Barrett agree with respect to Koticomota and Pipoholma. Netstul, Owotelpeti, and Unutsawaholma may be considered to have replaced Cimela and Koloko. The status of Tsimitutsonoma, as indicated above, is dubious, in spite of the fact that Driver's informants gave it as a permanent town. In view of the doubt it is better to omit it from consideration.

Directing our attention now to the six sure towns of Driver, we find in his paper some very pertinent data with regard to their size and demographic characteristics. The sizes and house numbers given (Driver, 1936) are:

Koticomota: "large town"; 2 sweathouses.

Netstul: "large town"; 40 houses; 1 sweathouse.

Owotelpete: 40 houses; 1 sweathouse.

Pipoholma: 40 houses; 1 sweathouse.

Unutsawaholmanoma: 1 sweathouse; 11 houses in 1870; 17 houses "formerly."

Osoyukeju: "small town"; 1 sweathouse.

Before discussing the house numbers in detail we should call attention to Driver's analysis of the village Unutsawa-holma-noma. This analysis (1936, pp. 201 ff.) he says is based upon "concrete genealogical census data of about the year 1870." There can therefore be no argument concerning the validity of the figures he presents. He found, in brief, that in this village there were 11 houses, containing 21 families and 92 persons. The occupants per house ranged from 4 to 21 with an average of 9, the families from 1 to 6 per house with an average of 2 (actually 1.91), and the persons per family averaged 4.5 (actually 4.38).

When we examined Gifford's figures for the Clear Lake Pomo village of Cigom we found 5.0 persons per family, 2.35 families per house, and 11.75 persons per house. The similarity between the two sets of values, derived by different investigators independently, is clearly significant. Moreover, the slightly smaller numbers discovered by Driver at Unutsawaholma are explicable on the basis of the later date (1870) taken as the base line. At any rate there can be no doubt that the two villages were remarkably alike in composition of population.

In computing aboriginal population at Cigom and the surrounding country it was pointed out that Gifford actually was dealing with a *declining* population and that, if the aboriginal state were to be conceived properly, his figures would have to be increased. For this reason the family number was set at 7 instead of 5, which raised the number of persons per house to 16.45. Because of other evidence the latter value was reduced to 14.0.

For Driver's village the same considerations must apply. However, since the family number was found to be 4.38, rather than 5.0 the aboriginal value may be put at 6 instead of 7. Then, if the number of families per house is 1.91, the average persons per house would be 11.5, a figure which there is no strong reason for changing. It now appears that, if Unutsawaholma "formerly" had 17 houses, with 11.5 persons per house, the "former" population would have been approximately 195, or in round numbers 200.

Returning the matter of houses, Driver says that his informants "estimated" the number, but he thought the estimates were too high. (The number for the village of Unutsawaholma was evidently known exactly.) I think we have to concede Driver's point but we still do not know how great was the exaggeration. We note that Unutsawaholma with 17 sure houses "formerly" had 1 sweathouse but no designation "large" or "small." Of the two "large towns" one had 2 sweathouses and the other had 1 sweathouse and 40 ordinary houses. The same numbers were assigned to two other villages but they were not called large or small. The one called "small" had 1 sweathouse. The village, therefore, with 1 sweathouse and 17 other houses, but not designated either large or small, may be taken as approximately intermediate. The small town may be assigned half this number, or 8 houses. Those with 40 estimated houses, but not called large, may be assigned 25 houses each. Netstul, a "large town" with 40 houses and 1 sweathouse, may be given 30 houses, and Koticomota, a "large town" with 2 sweathouses, may be given 35 houses. This is a purely arbitrary arrangement but it must come somewhere near fitting the facts.

On this basis we have six villages with a total of 140 houses and an average of nearly 23. This would mean an aboriginal population of 1,610 persons. If we were to admit no declining population in 1870 but if we allowed that Unutsawaholma, with 17 houses, was of average size in aboriginal times, the value would still be 1,010 for the population of Alexander Valley.

Driver states, in conjunction with his village list, "these certainly not all inhabited at the same time." His opinion may be justified but he cites no evidence in its support, and the circumstantial data brought out with respect to each village separately does not indicate that discontinuance of habitation occurred very long ago. It is true that Alexander Valley was the scene of a minor intertribal war in the early years of the nineteenth century, as the result of which the Pomo were driven out by the Wappo. In the confusion there may have been some shifting of inhabitants and reconstitution of villages, with the consequence that the population came to include both racial elements. Nevertheless, the data presented by Driver imply a total number of inhabitants, at one time, of fully 1,610. If Barrett's eighth village, Tekenantsonoma, on Sulphur Creek, is allowed 70 inhabitants, the total is raised to 1,680.

The Northern Wappo and the Lake Miwok form the next natural division. It is preferable to treat these two groups together, and more or less in defiance of strict tribal limits, because the precise boundary between the Wappo and the Lake Miwok has never yet been determined to the entire satisfaction of ethnographers and because the racial affiliation of certain villages is still open to doubt. Bypassing the ethnographic problem, therefore, we may consider the area south of Clear Lake, which includes the headwaters of Putah Creek and upper Pope Valley. The region embraces a rough triangle, the apices of which are the modern villages of Lower Lake, Pope Valley, and Middletown.

The ethnographic sources consist of the works of Merriam, Barrett, and Kroeber. Merriam covered what he considered to be the Lake Miwok in a manuscript entitled "Tu-le-yo-mi Tribe List" and the pertinent Wappo villages in a manuscript entitled "Yukean." Barrett (1908) devoted several pages to the Wappo and to the Lake Miwok Kroeber's discussion in the Handbook was based largely upon these authorities but he later amplified his views in his paper (1932, pp. 366-369) on "The Patwin and Their Neighbors." Since all three investigators have contributed village lists, it will be necessary to examine them in detail. Previously, however, one particular problem requires brief mention.

Within the area of the Lake Miwok and Northern Wappo there was once a village or a pair of villages, the names and locations of which have been the source of much controversy. Barrett (1908, p. 273) mentioned "*loknoma*, from lok, goose, and noma, village, or *lakah-yome* ... at a point about three-quarters of a mile northeast of Middletown...." Continuing the discussion at some length, Barrett finally suggests the possibility that these people lived on the Locollomillo Rancho in Pope Valley.

Kroeber (1932, p. 366) found an informant who distinguished between Loknoma and Lakah-yomi as two separate towns, both near Middletown. Kroeber remarks: "Apparently the two 'capitals' Lok-noma and Lakah-yomi stood close together, while their territories stretched apart, a condition for which there is precedent." On his general map (1932, back cover) he places

Lok-noma almost at Middletown in Northern Wappo territory and Lakah-yomi just to the north in the realm of the Lake Miwok.

Meanwhile Merriam, in his "Tu-le-yo-mi Tribe List," specifies two rancherias. One is called Al-lok-yo-me-po-goot and is in Pope Valley, whereas the other, at Middletown, is Lah-ki-yo-me-po-goot. Merriam, furthermore, reinforces his distinction by citing numerous Spanish synonyms which he collected from the mission records. Thus for Al-lok-yo-me-po-goot he mentions Alacyomi, Aloquiomi, Alocyome, and Aloqui. For Lah-ki-yo-me-po-goot he gives Laoquiomi, Laoquio, Locollomillos, Laknomah, Locnoma, and Locolomne. The presence or absence of the initial letter *a* appears to have been the deciding criterion, according to those who wrote in Spanish.

On the whole it is probable, as Kroeber concluded, that two towns are involved. One undoubtedly was near Middletown. The other may have been near by, as stated by Kroeber, or it may have been in Pope Valley, as suggested by Merriam. Fortunately we are not called upon to make a decision since, for population estimates, it becomes irrelevant where the exact locations were. The evidence is adequate that there were in fact two important villages, of very similar name, lying within the consolidated territory of the Lake Miwok and the Northern Wappo.

We may now examine the village lists of Merriam, Barrett, and Kroeber. All references to Kroeber are to his monograph of 1932.

> *Al-lok-yo-me-po-goot* (Merriam). Refer to preceding discussion.
>
> *Lah-ki-yo-me-po-goot* (Merriam), *Loknoma* (Barrett). Refer to preceding discussion.
>
> *Tu-le-yo-me-po-goot* (Merriam). *Tuleyome* (Barrett), *Tule-yomi* (Kroeber). This is widely known as the largest village of the Lake Miwok.
>
> *O-la-yo-me-po-goot* (Merriam), *Oleyome* (Barrett), *Ole-yomi* (Kroeber). This village is also known as having been large and important.
>
> *Wen-nok* (Merriam), *Guenoc* (Barrett), *Guenoc* (Kroeber). Considerable mystery surrounds this name, although it has been known and used for nearly one hundred years. Barrett says that the Indians never employed the name but that it referred to a subtribe, or group associated with the Oleyome. Kroeber says that "it was admitted as a native name, but untranslated." He thinks it may be identical with *Wilok-yomi*,

a village mentioned by his informant. Merriam says it was either (1) the name of a lake the valley of which contained three rancherias or (2) on Oleyome band, located 4 miles northeast of Middletown. In view of the wide divergence of opinion the safest procedure is to consider the Guenoc as simply constituting a portion of the Oleyome.

Kah-we-yo-me (Merriam), *Kahweyome* (Barrett), *Kawi-yomi* (Kroeber). Merriam says the village was located on Cache Creek, as do Barrett and Kroeber. Kroeber says: "My informant did not refer to the two sites mentioned here by Barrett, Tsitsa-pukut and Kawi-yomi, and when asked about the former replied that some of the Miwok had drifted there, presumably in later years." If Kroeber's informant was correct, then both Barrett's villages are postaboriginal and must be omitted from further consideration.

Shoyome (Merriam), *Coyome* (Barrett), *Kai-yomi-pukut* (Kroeber). This town is placed by all three authorities on Putah Creek, and hence is to be distinguished clearly from the preceding town, Kah-we-yo-me. Furthermore it was known to the pre-American Californians as Coyayomi, Joyayomi, or Cauyomi. Its aboriginal existence seems established.

Pe-te-no-mah (Merriam), *Petinoma* (Barrett). This village is placed on upper Putah Creek by both Merriam and Barrett; hence its existence is probable.

Holilelemona (Merriam), *Holilelenoma* (Barrett). Barrett says this was a camp site.

Koo-pa-choo (Merriam, MS "Yukean"), *Kupetcu* (Barrett). Barrett says this was a camp site.

Uyuhanoma (Barrett). *Yawi-yomi-pukut* (Kroeber). Both authors place this village near Middletown. Its existence is highly probable.

Hoo-koo-yo-me-po-koot (Merriam). *Hukuyome* or *Siwiyome* (Barrett). Barrett says that this village was established in 1835 by survivors from Oleyome. It is therefore not aboriginal.

Ka-bool-po-goot (Merriam). *Kebulpukut* (Barrett). *Tubud* or *Tubul* (Kroeber). Existence highly probable since it is mentioned by three investigators.

Kah-dah-yo-me (Merriam), *Kadoi-yomi-pukut* (Kroeber). Existence probable.

Kil-le-yo-ke-po-koot (Merriam), *Kilinyoke* (Kroeber). Existence probable.

Lahl-mok-po-goot (Merriam), *Lalmak-pukut* (Kroeber). Existence probable.

Lu-pu-yo-me (Merriam). No details are given by Merriam but the existence of the village is rendered very probable by the fact that 57 persons are recorded as having been baptized at the mission of San Rafael from *Lupuyome*. The village may have been destroyed in the process of conversion and hence have been unknown to later informants.

Sahl-sahl-po-goot (Merriam), *Shalshal-pukut* (Kroeber). Existence probable.

Sah-ti-yo-me-po-goot (Merriam). This village is mentioned by no other investigator but there are recorded baptisms at Solano Mission from *Tsatiyome*, which is undoubtedly the same name, hence its existence is highly probable.

Tsit-sah-yome (Merriam), *Tsitsapogut* (Barrett), *Tsitsa-pukut* (Kroeber). This village must be omitted because of the doubt cast by Kroeber's informant. See Ka-we-yo-me.

Tso-ke-yo-me-po-goot (Merriam), *Tsok-yomi-pokut* (Kroeber). Existence probable.

Tumistumis (Barrett), *Tumistumis-pukut* (Kroeber). Existence probable.

Wo-de-di-tep-pe-po-goot (Merriam), *Wodidaitepi* (Kroeber). Existence probable.

Al-lok-ko-boo-je (Merriam only). Existence possible.

Al-lok-woo-boo-te (Merriam only). Existence possible.

Haw-hawl-po-goot (Merriam only). Existence possible.

Hol-wah-poo-koot (Merriam only). Existence possible.

Oo-yoo-hah-no-mah (Merriam only). Existence possible.

Kalau-yomi (Kroeber only). Existence possible.

Kitsin-pukut (Kroeber only). Existence possible.

Shanak-yomi-pukut (Kroeber only). Existence possible.

Tsukeliwa-pukut (Kroeber only). Existence possible.

Reviewing the above compilation, we find four villages the existence, size, and importance of which are beyond reasonable doubt. There are five the names of which were known to the informants of all three ethnographers, or can be found in the mission records. Hence their existence can be accepted without serious question. Eight others were located by two, but not three, ethnographers. The probability of their actual, aboriginal existence is not high but on the other hand there is no clear reason for excluding them. Four can be omitted from further consideration on the ground that they were camp sites or were founded after 1850. Nine are reported by only one investigator, and therefore all confirmation of their status is lacking. It is quite unlikely that each of these was a permanent aboriginal village. On the other hand, the fact that even one informant remembered the name is presumptive evidence for existence of some sort. As a purely empirical device, in order to settle the matter, let us assume that each of the nine names represents a small village of 20 inhabitants.

With respect to the size of the villages we suffer from a complete lack of any direct information. By comparison with the rancherias around Clear Lake and in Alexander Valley we could consider that the four large towns contained 200 persons apiece. The five highly probable villages are likely to have been larger than many others, and may have contained 100 each. To the eight reasonably sure, but by no means certain, places we may ascribe 50 persons each. The nine doubtful ones can certainly be covered by a total of 200. The aggregate, then, is 1,900.

In default of further ethnographic help we must fall back on mission data. In the records of San Francisco, Solano, and San Rafael it is possible to find baptisms assigned to the following recognized villages: Coyome, Loknoma (Lah-ki-yo-me-po-goot), Aloquiomi (Al-lok-yo-me-po-goot), Oleyome, Tuleyome, and Lupuyome. These names are no doubt more or less generic in character in that the missionaries were using them to apply to the larger villages or even subtribes. We would not expect them to conform in detail to any of the lists supplied by modern ethnographers. The total baptism number may, however, be taken as covering the area as a whole.

The Lake Miwok (together with the Clear Lake Pomo) and the Northern Wappo were the most remote people, north of the Bay, who were reached for conversion prior to the secularization of the missions. All activity in this area was confined to the period 1824-1834, and was carried on by necessity through well organized, semimilitary, semireligious expeditions. Owing to unavoidable obstacles it was possible to get physical possession of and bring back to the missions only a small proportion of the potential converts. The exact value of this proportion can never be known, and indeed it undoubtedly varied widely from place to place. A similar question arose in connection with a previous study of the population of the San Joaquin Valley. For the latter area the conditions were postulated that the site of native residence was several score miles from the nearest mission, that a formally organized expedition had to be undertaken, and that there was able and determined opposition to missionization on the part of the natives. Under such circumstances it was concluded on the basis of evidence available that a fair approximation to the proportion of natives actually baptized was 15 per cent of the existing population. In most respects the situation south and southeast of Clear Lake was very similar to that obtaining in the lower San Joaquin Valley and the delta region. Hence the indicated baptism factor may be employed here.

For the six major subdivisions mentioned above the total baptisms at Solano and San Rafael were 264. If this number represents 15 per cent, the population was 1,760, a value not basically different from the arbitrary figure derived from the village lists. An intermediate estimate, 1,800, will be taken for the population of the Lake Miwok and Northern Wappo.

For the Central Wappo there is a paucity of ethnographic data. Furthermore the territory itself is very circumscribed, since Pope Valley has been allocated for present purposes to the Northern Wappo and embraces little more than the flat land within a radius of a few miles from the modern town of Calistoga. Merriam cites only one name (in the manuscript entitled "Yukean"), viz., *Mi-yahk-ma*. Barrett (1908, p. 269) gives *Maiyakma*, together with *Nilektsonoma* and *Tselmenan*, which were close by. In addition he lists *Mitustul*, five miles to the west of Calistoga. It seems likely that we have here a single small division, or tribelet, with the "capital" at Maiyakma and with three smaller, peripheral villages. If we use the same population estimates as we did farther north, we may ascribe 200 persons to Maiyakma and 100 each to the others, making 500 in all.

The mission records supply two items of interest. The first is a note from Sonoma that there were baptized 103 persons from Mayacma "ó Tamalsimas." The latter name is probably a corruption of the term written by Barrett as Tselmenan, and indicates that this village was then in existence. The other item is from San Rafael which reported 9 baptisms from Teluasuenhuca "ó Tamalsimela." The total then is 112.

The baptism factor of 15 per cent cannot be used here with confidence because the upper Napa Valley was much more accessible to the San Rafael Mission and particularly the Sonoma Mission than was the area around and above Middletown. At the same time the distance and difficulty of approach were somewhat greater than in the case of the lower Russian River Valley near Santa Rosa and Sebastopol, for which the baptism factor was taken as one-third. As a compromise we may take a factor of one-quarter, or 25 per cent. This yields an estimated population of 450, a figure which appears not unreasonable.

For the Southern Wappo Merriam mentions Guiluc (MS "Yukean") and Kaimus. The latter is very well known and is discussed by Barrett (1908,). The former is in territory which was disputed between the Pomo and the Wappo and may be either *wilikos* (Wappo) or *Wilok* (Pomo)—see Barrett's treatment of the Ethnogeography (1908). For present purposes it may be considered as Wappo since it was excluded from the Pomo in computing the population of the latter group. Merriam cites no other names, but Barrett gives Annakotonoma and Tsemanoma among the Southern Wappo (1908, p. 269) and Tcimenukme, Tuluka, and Suskol as Wintun villages at the mouth of Napa River. Annakotonoma was known to the missionaries as Callajomanos (and variants), Guiluc as such, and Kaimus as Caymus (and variants). The three Wintun villages have left no trace whatever in the mission records under Barrett's names or any recognizable variants. This is rather surprising, since the area was thoroughly converted by the missionaries at San Rafael and at Sonoma. Very likely the baptisms are in the record but under designations (and there are many) which do not permit the allocation to a specific tribe or village. On the other hand, the area itself is probably included in the appellation "Napa" which appears to have covered the entire region from the present city of Napa to the shore of the Bay.

The sum of the recorded baptisms from Caymus, Guiluc, Callajomanos, and Napa is 331. A baptism factor of 25 per cent cannot be employed because the territory of these groups was very close to the Sonoma Mission, and from numerous accounts by contemporary writers we know that missionization was nearly complete. A factor of 50 per cent would give a probable population of 662 and one of 75 per cent a population of 442. Both values are evidently too low.

The final resource from which we may seek information is provided by the accounts of the early American settlers. Chief of these is George Yount, who entered Napa Valley in 1831 and took up a grant of land near the present town of Yountville. Yount seems to have been a sober and reliable citizen, and one who was accorded the respect of his fellow pioneers. His story consists of a series of verbal recollections which were written down in manuscript form by a friend, the Rev. Orange Clark, who visited his ranch in 1851. The Clark manuscript, together with other material, has been secured and published by Professor Charles L. Camp (1923).

Yount seems to have discoursed at length on the local Indians (1923, p. 55). His description of the tribes follows (I have omitted the explanatory parentheses inserted by Camp).

> "Within a distance of no more than One Hundred miles in length & twenty in width, including the Napa Valley, were five distinct nations, no one of which could converse together ... without an interpreter ... The names of these five nations were as follows—The Napa, the Ouluke, Caymus, Conahomanes & Miacamus, the last named tribe inhabited the region of the Hot Springs of that valley...."

Four of these names are clear. The fifth, Ouluke, is very probably Tuluka of Barrett. Since these five groups are sharply defined by the Napa Valley and since Yount obviously was talking about that area, his size estimate was excessive. He says 100 miles by 20, whereas the valley actually is about 40 miles in length from the Bay to Mt. St. Helena and perhaps on the average 15 miles in width, from the crest of one range across to the other.

With regard to numbers Yount says (1923, p. 56):

> "It is not yet eight years [evidently referring to the year 1843] since the above named valley swarmed with not less than eight thousand human beings, of whom there are not now [1851] left as many hundreds.... The poor remnants of all the five tribes above named now mingle & wander up and down the valley promiscuously together...."

There is also an account of the destruction of the Caymus (1923, p. 59). A great many, if not most of them, were killed by being burnt in a sweathouse. The guilty parties were stated to be two Indians from San Rafael, but the motives were obscure. This event occurred some time during the later days of Yount's tenure, for, continues the manuscript, "at a period long previous to the tragical event above related, Yount embarked in erecting a small flour mill...."

Although Alexander Taylor, in his Indianology, mentions some of the subtribes of the Wappo, he gives no useful population data. On the other hand, John S. Hittell talked about the Napa Valley Indians in an article in the Hesperian Magazine entitled Notes on Napa Valley (1860, p. 55). He gives the same tribes, or subtribes, as were mentioned by Yount in the manuscript edited by Camp. These were the Mayacomas, the Callajomanas, the Caymus, the Napa Indians, the Soscol, and the Ulacas. He then adds the following:

> Their rancherias were numerous throughout the length of
> the valley.... It is not known how many of these Indians there
> were, no census having been taken nor any careful estimate
> having been made, at the time, by anybody. Mr. Yount
> thinks their number was not less than three thousand, and
> possibly twice as many. It would have been an easy matter
> to collect a thousand warriors in those times.

Shortly afterward C. A. Menefee (1873) wrote a history of Napa and adjacent counties, using Hittell and Alexander Taylor as his only written authorities. No historical scholar in the professional sense, Menefee nevertheless devoted a full chapter to the Napa Valley Indians, and gives evidence of having undertaken to secure such information as he could from local residents. His statements are not sensational and appear within reasonable limits to be reliable.

He lists the six tribes exactly as does Hittell. He expands on Hittell's quotation from Yount thus (1873, p. 19): Yount said that "in round numbers there were from 10,000 to 12,000 Indians ranging the country between Napa and Clear Lake. Of this number he [Yount] says there were at least 3,000 in Napa County, and perhaps twice that number." At one point Menefee comments (1873, p. 18): "No estimate of their [Indians'] numbers appears to have been made until 1823, and it was known that they had then greatly decreased."

Menefee's principal contribution, however, is a rough computation of the surviving Indian population in 1843. This estimate occurs nowhere else to my knowledge, and I think was no doubt secured by Menefee through personal interviews with early settlers. He says (1873, p. 18) that there were 50 to 100 Indians on the Bale rancho, 400 at Caymus rancho, 600 at Salvador rancho, a "large number" at Soscol. Amplifying this count, he says: "It was the custom of the Indians to establish their rancherias upon the grants of the early settlers, in order to gain a livelihood by occasional labor." Also: "These were in some sense permanently fixed and residing constantly in one place. Besides these there were thousands of nomads, who roamed the valleys and mountains...."

Menefee also describes the destruction of an Indian community, the Callajomanas. This time it was a group of white ranchers from Sonoma Valley who became incensed at stock depredations, came to the village, and slaughtered 300 Indians—according to Menefee—as they emerged from a sweathouse. Whether this tale is confused with the account of Yount on the Caymus tragedy is difficult to say. The circumstances and the number of Indians involved may well be garbled, but that some such incident took place is highly probable.

If we now confine the area in question to Napa Valley, as all these persons clearly intended, we are dealing with the Central Wappo, the Southern Wappo, and the Wintun on Napa River. The best guess from the mission records for the population is about 1,800. To allow an area of 15 by 40 square miles and the maximum Pomo density of 8 persons per square mile would yield a population of 4,800. Yount said, according to Clark, as transmitted by Camp (1923, p. 56), that the valley "swarmed" with not less than 8,000 people in 1843. Yount, by way of Hittell and Menefee (1873, p. 19), put 10,000 to 12,000 from Napa to Clear Lake and 3,000 or "perhaps twice that number" in Napa Valley alone. It is clear that Yount was not a very accurate reporter and in default of actual knowledge made a broad guess. Yet I doubt greatly if Yount would have put the number in thousands—no matter how many—if there had actually been only a few hundred or a few score Indians in the country at the time of his arrival. The presence of a number approximating his low guess, 3,000, is not out of line with probability.

Let us turn to Menefee. His figures for 1843 were organized according to ranches. Furthermore let it be noted that, according to his explicit statement, the aboriginal village organization had broken down utterly, and the Indians were living in new places in conformity with new economic and social requirements. No wonder modern informants frequently cannot look past the period of upheaval and give us a clear picture of untouched aboriginal life before the white man came!

Regarding the accuracy of the figures, specifically the three items for which literal numbers are given, it can be said again, as was pointed out with reference to J. B. R. Cooper, that a ranch owner should have known roughly how many Indians were living in his own back yard. If we refuse to accept these estimates, then we had better be prepared to reject most historical testimony. We may then base our calculation on 75 Indians for the Bale ranch, 400 for the Caymus ranch, and 600 for the Salvador ranch. The Juarez and the Higuera ranches contained a "large number." Since the largest number actually given is 600, we may with safety consider that 300 would represent a "large number." A "still larger number" could reasonably be 400. The total then becomes 2,075. Menefee, however, is careful to state that this included only the Indians who were "in some sense" permanently located, and puts the unattached number in the "thousands." The latter can of course be scaled down drastically. Hundreds would be a good substitute, with a possible total of one thousand. The outcome then is that the Indian population of Napa Valley as a whole in 1843 was about 3,000, or identical with Yount's minimum estimate.

What was, now, the population aboriginally? The mission baptisms are of no use to us since the Indians in 1843 included most of the ex-neophytes in the area. That there had already been a profound reduction at that time is unquestioned. The north shore of the Bay had been subject to military, clerical, and civilian incursion since the beginning of the century. Lethal epidemics had swept over the country repeatedly. Massacre and slaughter had been the rule rather than the exception. Indeed, the open valley through Sonoma and Napa up to Calistoga had suffered more seriously than any other area except perhaps the delta of the Sacramento River. A population reduction from the aboriginal level by one-third prior to 1843 would not be out of line with the apparent facts.

The estimates for the period 1840-1845 derived from Yount, Hittell, and Menefee included the Central Wappo with the more southern groups. For the Central Wappo the ethnographic sources and the mission records indicated an aboriginal population of 450 or 500. However, it is probably advisable to disregard this small division as a separate entity and include it with the remaining Wappo and the Suscol Wintun. If we then take Yount's minimum estimate of 3,000 for the Napa Valley south of Mt. St. Helena and if we assume a one-third decrease in numbers from aboriginal times to 1843, the final estimate for the area becomes 4,500.

The figure just derived is of course considerably greater than would be indicated by either the ethnographic village lists or the mission baptism records, but it must be conceded that the two last methods of approach are inadequate for the situation existing in the Napa Valley. On the other hand for a population of 4,500 and an area of 600 square miles, the density would be 7.5 persons per square mile, or very close to the value arrived at for the near-by Pomo.

We have found by ethnographic derivation 1,680 persons for the Western Wappo and 1,800 for the Northern Wappo and Lake Miwok together. Thus the total for the Lake Miwok, the Wappo, and the Suscol Wintun as a whole becomes approximately 8,000.

WAPPO, LAKE MIWOK, AND NAPA VALLEY WINTUN ... 8,000

SUMMARY OF ESTIMATES

For convenience of reference the population estimates presented in the foregoing text are tabulated as follows:

Yurok		3,100
Wiyot		3,300
Karok		2,700
Hupa		2,000
Tolowa		2,400
Athapascans		
Chilula	800	
Mattole	1,200	
Whilkut	1,300	
Kato	1,100	
Lassik	1,500	
Nongatl	3,300	
Sinkyone	2,900	
Wailaki	3,350	
Total		15,450
Yuki		
Coast Yuki	750	
Yuki proper	6,880	
Huchnom	2,100	
Total		9,730
Pomo		
Clear Lake Pomo	3,150	
Northern Pomo	5,040	
Central and Southwestern Pomo	6,220	
Southern Pomo	6,000	
Northeastern Pomo	350	
Total		20,760

Coast Miwok	3,000
Wappo, Lake Miwok, Napa Valley Wintun	8,000
GRAND TOTAL	70,440

BIBLIOGRAPHY

Abbreviations

AA	American Anthropologist, Menasha, Wis.
BAE-B	Bureau of American Ethnology, Smithsonian Institution, Bulletin
UC	University of California Publications, Berkeley and Los Angeles
–AR	Anthropological Records
–IA	Ibero-Americana
–PAAE	American Archaeology and Ethnology

Barrett, S. A.

1908.   The Ethno-Geography of the Pomo and Neighboring Indians. UC-PAAE, Vol. 6.

Bledsoe, A. J.

1885.   Indian Wars of the Northwest. San Francisco.

California, State of

1860.   Majority and Minority Reports of the Special Joint Committee on the Mendocino War. Appendix to Journals of the Assembly of the Eleventh Session of the California Legislature, 1860.

Camp, C. L.

1923.   The Chronicles of George C. Yount. In Calif. Hist. Soc. Quarterly, 2: 3-66.

Cook, S. F.

1943.   The Conflict Between the California Indian and White Civilization: I. UC-IA No. 21.

Driver, H. E.

1936.   Wappo Ethnography. UC-PAAE 36: 179-220.

Drucker, Philip.

1937.   The Tolowa and Their Southwest Oregon Kin. UC-PAAE 36: 221-300.

Foster, G. M.

1944.   A Summary of Yuki Culture. UC-AR 5: 155-244.

Gibbs, George.

1860.   Journal of the Expedition of Colonel Redick M'Kee ... in 1851. In Henry R. Schoolcraft, Archives of Aboriginal Knowledge, 3: 99-177.

Gifford, E. W.

1923.   Pomo Lands on Clear Lake. UC-PAAE 20: 77-92.

1926.   Clear Lake Pomo Society. UC-PAAE 18: 287-390.

1939.   The Coast Yuki. Anthropos, 34: 292-375.

Gifford, E. W., and A. L. Kroeber

1937.   Culture Element Distributions: Pomo. UC-PAAE 37: 117-254.

Goddard, P. E.

1903.   The Life and Culture of the Hupa. UC-PAAE 1: 1-88.

1914.   Notes on the Chilula Indians of Northwestern California. UC-PAAE 10: 265-288.

1923.   The Habitat of the Wailaki. UC-PAAE 20: 95-112.

1924.   The Habitat of the Pitch Indians, a Wailaki Division. UC-PAAE 17: 217-225.

Heintzelman, H. P.

1855.   Report dated San Francisco, Nov. 17, 1855. Original in U.S. National Archive, Office of Indian Affairs, Record Group no. 75, Letters Received, California, 1855. Enclosure to Doc. no. H 1100.

Hittell, J. S.

1860.   Notes on Napa Valley. In the Hesperian Magazine. 4: 53-61.

Kniffen, F. B.

    1939.   Pomo Geography. UC-PAAE 36: 353-400.

Kroeber, Alfred L.

    1925.   Handbook of the Indians of California, BAE-B 78, Washington, D.C.

    1932.   The Patwin and Their Neighbors. UC-PAAE 29: 253-423.

    1936.   Karok Towns. UC-PAAE 35: 29-38.

Loud, L. L.

    1918.   Ethnogeography and Archaeology of the Wiyot Territory. UC-PAAE 14: 221-436.

Menefee, C. A.

    1873.   Historical and Descriptive Sketch Book of Napa, Sonoma, Lake and Mendocino ... Reporter Publishing House, Napa City, Calif.

Merriam, C. Hart.

    Dates uncertain. Village Lists. Manuscripts in the possession of the Department of Anthropology, University of California, Berkeley.

    After the decease of the late C. Hart Merriam his heirs generously made available to the Department of Anthropology of the University of California, Berkeley, a large and valuable collection of Dr. Merriam's notes on California Indians. Among these papers are to be found complete and very carefully recorded lists of villages for most of the California tribes, drawn not only from published sources but also from original information secured from informants on the scene. Much material, otherwise unavailable, has thus been secured. These documents are referred to in this text simply as the Village Lists of C. Hart Merriam or are cited by Merriam's own manuscript title. They are undated and a formal bibliographical reference in most cases cannot be given.

    1905.   The Indian Population of California. AA 7: 594-606.

M'Kee, John.

    1853.   Minutes Kept by John M'Kee, Secretary on the Expedition from Sonoma, through Northern California. 33rd Cong. spec. sess. Sen. Ex. Doc. no. 4, pp. 134-180.

Nomland, G. A.

    1935.   Sinkyone Notes. UC-PAAE 36: 149-178.

    1938.   Bear River Ethnography. UC-AR 2: 91-126.

Nomland, G. A., and A. L. Kroeber

    1936.   Wiyot Towns. UC-PAAE 35: 39-48.

Palmer, L. L.

    1881.   History of Napa and Lake Counties. Slocum, Bowen and Co., San Francisco.

Powers, S.

    1877.   Tribes of California. Contributions to North American Ethnology, Vol. 3.

Stewart, O. C.

    1943.   Notes on Pomo Ethnogeography. UC-PAAE 40: 29-62.

Taylor, A. S.

    1860-1863.   The Indianology of California.

                Published as a series of articles by the California Farmer. The entire series has been clipped and pasted in a bound volume available at the Bancroft Library, Berkeley.

Waterman, T. T.

    1920.   Yurok Geography. UC-PAAE 16: 177-314.

    1925.   Village Sites in Tolowa and Neighboring Areas of Northwestern California. AA 27: 528-543.

9 789359 953885